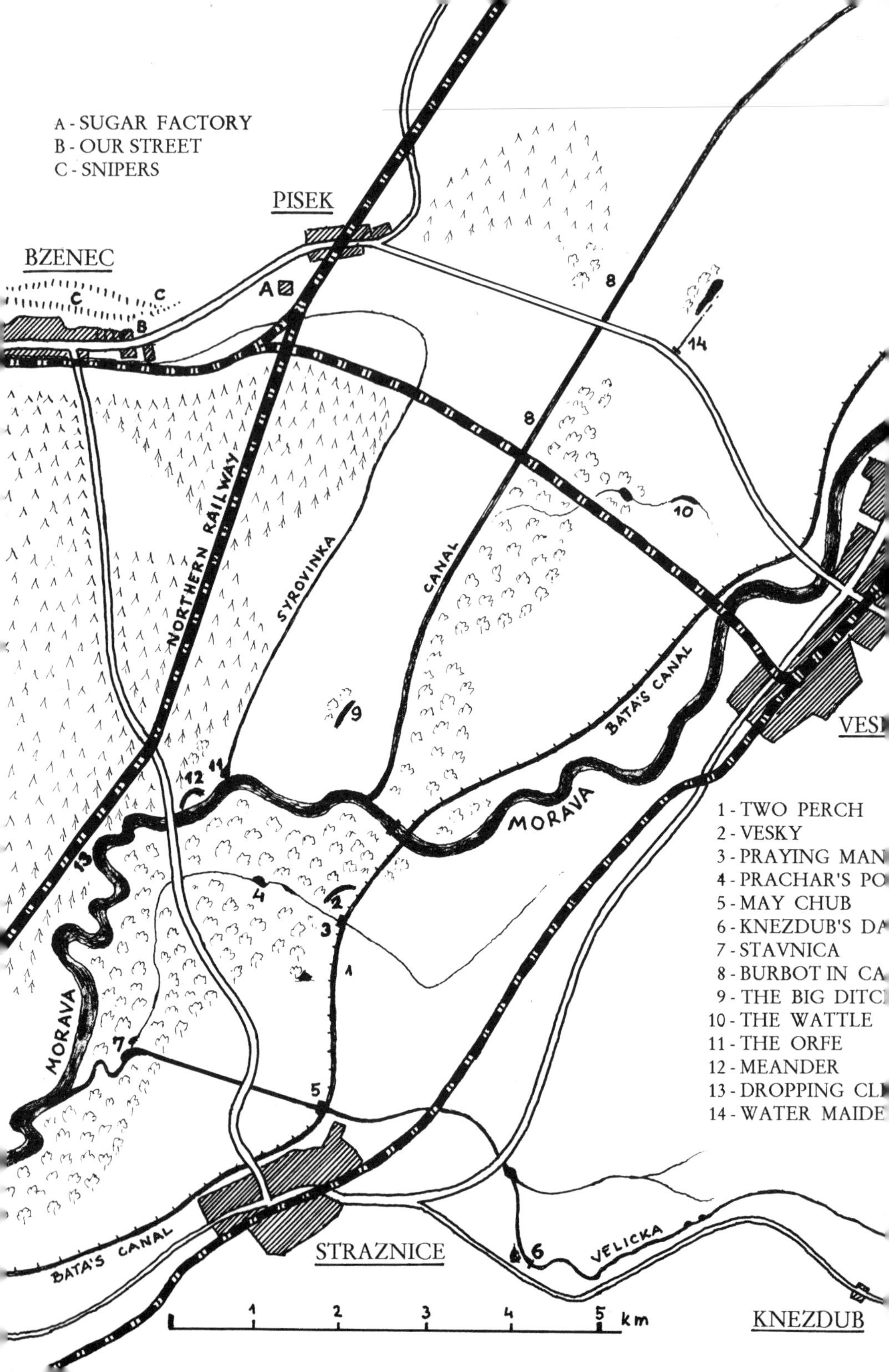

A - SUGAR FACTORY
B - OUR STREET
C - SNIPERS
PISEK
BZENEC
NORTHERN RAILWAY
SYROVINKA
CANAL
BATA'S CANAL
MORAVA
MORAVA
VES
1 - TWO PERCH
2 - VESKY
3 - PRAYING MAN
4 - PRACHAR'S PO
5 - MAY CHUB
6 - KNEZDUB'S DA
7 - STAVNICA
8 - BURBOT IN CA
9 - THE BIG DITC
10 - THE WATTLE
11 - THE ORFE
12 - MEANDER
13 - DROPPING CL
14 - WATER MAIDE
VELICKA
BATA'S CANAL
STRAZNICE
KNEZDUB
1
2
3
4
5 km

Oldrich Misa

UNDER THE SIGN OF PISCES

II

First published in Great Britain
in 1995 by O. Misa,
Easter Sun, Orford, Suffolk IP12 2NU

ISBN 0 9524522 1 9

Printed and bound in Great Britain by
J.B. Offset Printers (Marks Tey) Ltd.,
Marks Tey, Colchester, Essex CO6 1EG

ESCAPES FROM

WAR

CONTENTS

PREFACE

The independent republic of Czechoslovakia which was created at the end of the First World War, on 28th October 1918, lasted for only twenty years. As a result of the agreement signed in Munich between Hitler's Nazi Germany and Great Britain, at the beginning of October 1938 Hitler's Nazi troops occupied our borderland - the so-called 'Sudetenland' - and thus destroyed the integrity of our State.

Until this time our family - consisting of my father (Tatinek), mother (Maminka), brother (Stana) 2 years older than I, and myself - had lived happily in Znojmo, the main town of South Moravia situated near the frontier with Austria and about 60 kms north of Vienna. Now we were forced to leave and move to the interior of our violently reduced Czechoslovakia.

The first fourteen years of my life, in the pre-Munich Republic, I have described in the first part of my memoirs 'CHILDHOOD', finishing with the day, 25th November 1938, when we loaded our furniture onto a small lorry and left the town of my birth, Znojmo.

This second part of my memoirs, 'ESCAPES FROM WAR', continues from the point of our crossing the newly created State frontier between Germany and the remnant of Czechoslovakia.

Seven years passed before we returned to Znojmo again. During this time Europe was groaning under the boots of Germany's Nazi forces and, as were the other countries, our crippled State was paying so dearly for Hitler's inhuman lunacy with human misery, suffering and lives.

At this time, which marked so painfully my growth and adolescence, I was escaping with my fishing rod to the waters where I could forget the distresses and hardships of war and find there instead thrilling pleasures, freedom and peace.

O. M.

1938

Leaving Znojmo - Searching for a new home - Moving to Straznice - Christmas fish

The target of our journey was Velke Pavlovice, the village where Tatinek's brother, my godfather Uncle Slavek, was employed in a similar position at the State wine research station as Tatinek had held in Znojmo. He had made an agreement with a local farmer that we could store our furniture in his barn.

The journey was simply terrible. The small lorry was so overloaded that at each bend it tilted so much the mudguards made the rubber tyres burn. Because we were afraid that the lorry could easily turn right over it was necessary to drive slowly, and soon pitch black night fell. In Pohorelice the driver left the main road and turned onto the narrow local roads, several times losing his way so that he had to go back again. After that the back tyre was punctured, luckily as we were going through a village, and the driver was able to stop the vehicle just in time so that it didn't overturn. As he had no spare wheel, the driver had to take off the damaged tyre and repair the punctured tube. He worked at it for ages, it was nearly midnight and freezing hard, and we were shaking with cold. At last we got moving again, but the repair didn't hold very well so we had to stop several times and pump air into the tube. Even when, during these compulsory halts we could leave the lorry, stretch our cramped limbs and, including Zolina the dog, answer the call of nature, we arrived at Pavlovice cold, stiff, shaken and sleepy, so we went straight to bed in our Uncle's house.

The furniture was unloaded only next day. Zolina had to stay with the farmer - our Uncle had a German Shepherd dog which was most unfriendly.

Tatinek went to the office in Brno to report on the handing over of the Znojmo office to the Germans and then went by train to Straznice where his new office was to be. He had been transferred to the Lower Agricultural School, but could not continue there with his expert professional work, that of a breeder of vines, instead being appointed as accountant. There was no flat for us at the School so he had to look for some cottage to rent or to buy where we could live.

At the town office nobody would help him, so he searched literally from house to house, unsuccessfully asking for possible accommodation for us and wasting the whole day. Next day somebody suggested he should go to the outskirts of the town where there was a street of new houses, and there he was stopped by some fat lady who greeted him in a very friendly fashion. Tatinek was most astonished that the lady, whom he had never seen before, called him by his name. But she insisted:

"Surely you remember me! You lived with us when you were practising in Mutenice!" It was true - in 1920, 18 years previously, Tatinek had been practising in Mutenice, but at that time he lived with the Srameks. Finally all was explained. Mrs Zabelka had mistaken

Tatinek for Uncle Slavek who, in his youth, looked very much like Tatinek and had been, during his practise in Mutenice, living with the Zabelkas.

Thanks to this unexpected and lucky meeting, Tatinek left the hotel and moved for a few days to the Zabelkas. Mr Zabelka was an officer with the gendarmes; they had one son, Jarka, who was in the 7th class of the Gymnasium and one daughter, Verka, who was in the lst class. Mrs Zabelka helped Tatinek in his search for some flat for us, but it was very difficult to find anything. At last she found, in the street 'Little cottages', lodgings with the Horaks in a farm, and a few days passed whilst the farmer cleared the rooms for us.

There was a narrow yard beside the buildings, while behind the yard and buildings was an orchard.

The part in which we were to live had only a kitchen and one room. The kitchen had been an old, damp cellar, with five steep steps leading down to it immediately behind the entrance door. The farm had no mains electricity and, because the kitchen was illuminated only through one window with only one very small pane of glass beside the door, the room was so dark that even during the day it had to be lit with a paraffin lamp. In the kitchen was a brick built range with a longish recess in the wall of the room beside it. Probably originally wood for the range had been stored there, but now it looked more like a place for laying a corpse, so I called it 'the tomb'. The floor of the kitchen was of flat stones and there were stairs rising from it to the second room which had two normal sized windows looking onto the street so this room was light. In the evenings, of course, even there we were using only the paraffin lamp. The floor was of wooden boards.

Both rooms had been used only for storing potatoes, beetroot and other things, they were filthy and had mouldy walls, so it was necessary to paint them with whitewash and added bluestone to kill the moulds and to scrape and wash the floors. At the same time Tatinek procured some wood and coal for heating, had a wooden closet made to put in the orchard behind the buildings, and was preparing the rooms for us to live there. This all needed so much time that the Zabelka's invited the whole of our family to stay with them for the time being.

We arrived at their house on 10th December, and the next day Stana and I went to be enrolled at the new Gymnasium so that we could continue with our studies which had been so cruelly interrupted. That meant a whole new environment for us, with new schoolmates and professors, and learning in extremely difficult conditions, all the lessons we had missed during the months when the school in Znojmo had been closed after the German occupation. It was most important to us that this new school accepted and recognized the first, mainly wasted, half term of our studies so that we would not have to repeat the whole year.

At the Zabelkas we had to improvise everything. There was not enough room in their small house for eight people. I was sleeping on the floor in the corridor, the others wherever it was possible. The fresh whitewash in our new home would not dry in the damp and cold weather, so Tatinek ordered two large steel baskets to be brought there, and in them we burned coke fires. On 20th December, just before Christmas, our most necessary pieces of furniture were delivered to us from Pavlovice, and at last we were able to move in.

Only one room was suitable to be lived in. We heated the living room with the small stove which had heated my parents' and our bedrooms in Znojmo. Our parents' beds and the ottoman on which Stana slept were put there, while the rest of the room was filled with four chairs and a table on which we had our meals and were doing our schoolwork. There was no room for my bed in it. I had to sleep, uncomfortably, in 'the tomb' in the kitchen - the recess in the wall beside the range. My mattress was a large sack filled with straw and my cover a feather eiderdown, with Tatinek's old fur coat over my legs. It was so damp that Maminka warmed my bed each evening with a hot roof tile, which she had heated on top of the small stove and wrapped in a towel.

There was such a poor draught for the kitchen range that it was always smoking, with the fire in it hardly burning at all so that Maminka had to add wood to the coal or she would never have been able to cook on it - even though she swept out the chimney every week! She so often talked about the excellent kitchen range she had had to leave behind in Znojmo!

Christmas was almost upon us. We knew that this time the holiday would be very poor, with no Christmas tree (for which there was no space in our room), no traditional carp (because in Straznice there was no shop which sold fish) and without gifts (because it was not possible to be looking for them under such conditions). But one gift we gave to each other after all. The day before Christmas Eve Stana went by train to Pavlovice, taking with him a small travelling basket. He said he wanted to bring back something. When he returned and opened the basket, out jumped our Zolina! Poor little dog - she was wild with excitement, squeaking, jumping up and licking us and, with all this excitement, piddling everywhere! We embraced her, and Maminka and I were both weeping, whilst Tatinek and Stana were deeply moved too. So it was a very happy Christmas after all. We ordered a new kennel for Zolina and put it in one of the empty stables.

During those first few days in Straznice I had already discovered with great satisfaction that there was some water there - the small river Velicka which filled the carp ponds in the castle park and Bata's canal along which lignite was transported from Ratiskovice to the shoe factories in Zlin. Near the small dam which restrained the waters for the canal I even saw a man fishing with a rectangular net suspended from the end of a long pole. Would he be there the next day, the afternoon of Christmas Eve?

When I came to the water the fisherman was there, on the same spot. He was fishing in the one place that was not yet covered with ice. I asked if he had caught anything, and he showed me his catch of not very large chub and bream.

At once there awoke in me the feelings which had been suppressed for the last five years. The wild fish were still much, much more beautiful than the small fish which we had had in our aquarium, so I stood beside the man and waited. At last he caught hold of the strong rope which was attached to the far end of the pole where there hung a crossbeam holding and stretching the net. He wedged his heels firmly against the frozen ground where the near end of the pole was jammed into the bank, leaned back with the full weight of his body and by pulling on the rope lifted the net from the water. There were only two small rudd in it, and the man lowered the net with the fish back into the water. About fifteen minutes passed before he lifted the net again, but this time it was empty. With a strong jerk he shook the water from it, took the pole with the net onto his shoulder and moved some 15 metres further along to the edge of the water which was not yet frozen, and there he once more tried his luck. After a longer interval he lifted his net again, and this time there were a good tench and three rudd in it. He took the tench and was about to return the rudd to the water, but I asked if I could have them, saying that I would like to have them for Christmas supper. While he was taking them out of the net the smallest dropped through, back into the water, but I at least had two! I tied the corners of my handkerchief together to make a carrier for the fish. The frost was growing stronger and ice was starting to form on the edges of the clear water. At the next lifting of the net there was one more rudd in it, which the fisherman again gave to me, and he wanted to go home. It was already so cold that the net above the water stiffened with frost in seconds. But I pleaded with him:

"Please try it once more, we are four at home!" It helped; he sank the net again into the water, the top of which was rapidly freezing. On the surface swordlike crystals were growing, crisscrossing each other and shooting sideways, and when the man lifted the net for the last time it was already full of sharp splinters and sheets of ice. But - there was another rudd there! The fourth! I thanked the man many times for it, and added it to the others which, in the time, had frozen solid in my handkerchief. I wished the man a merry Christmas and ran home. It was rapidly becoming dark.

When I arrived home, breathless, it was already completely dark, Maminka was very worried and nearly cross with me. Where had I been for such a long time?

But I laid my poor bundle very proudly on the table, and so we were able to have fish on Christmas Eve after all - even Zolina had a nibble of it. We were very happy that we were all together again in warmth, we forgot all our woes, and felt that perhaps, our worst troubles were now behind us.

The real winter started on Christmas Eve. Masses of snow fell, so that we often had to clear the path to the wooden closet in the orchard, and the frosts were so hard that at each opening of the door from the yard to the kitchen clouds of steam escaped and icy cold air rushed in. Each morning the inside of the door was covered with ice and icicles hung from it right down to the steps so that we had to beat the door and knock the icicles off or we could not have opened it. The stone floor, which we had covered with potato sacks, was all the same so cold that Maminka, when she was cooking, had her slippers bound with rags. The icy air lay just above the floor like water in a well. Later on the frost were stronger still so that even sacks nailed onto the inside of the door didn't help, and overnight the water in the bucket in the kitchen was frozen to ice.

There was no running water in the 'cottage', so we had to bring all our necessary supplies in buckets from the well in the street. Soon we learnt that when going for water it was wise to carry with us to the pump a quarter of a bucketful of warm water. The pump was so often frozen that it was not possible to move the handle. Only when we poured warm water down beside the piston rod inside the pump did it melt so that it was working again and we could fill our two big buckets. On Saturdays (bath night) it was necessary to bring six more bucketfuls.

In my 'tomb' a thick layer of hoarfrost grew on the low ceiling above me and on the bedding around my nose. If I lay quietly it was not so bad, but if I moved the touch of the hoarfrost would waken me. At last, when my nostrils were frostbitten, Tatinek concluded that I must move into their bedroom. Because there was no room for another bed we filled the gap between my parents' beds with rolled up towels and I slept with them. For none of us was it very comfortable.

1939

Pig killing - Maminka is ill - Studies - The new bicycle - End of the Republic - The mighty seven - I.Q. tests - Guarding the orchard - Vesky - Teacher of German - Moving house again - Prachar's pond

After the New Year there arrived from Polesovice a letter from Tatinek's sister, Aunt Johana, inviting Maminka to come and help with their pig killing. They had a pig weighing nearly 200 kilos, and to cope with such a quantity of meat every extra pair of hands was welcome. It is necessary to cut up the fat into small cubes and heat them to extract the lard, mix the blood for black puddings so that it does not coagulate, cut and mince pieces of meat, liver and boiled skin for liver sausages, boil pearl barley for black puddings, salt the bacon for smoking, and pickle meat with salt and garlic for later smoking. The smaller pieces of meat are cut up finely and are mixed with crushed garlic, paprika, black pepper, caraway seeds and salt for smoked sausages. The black puddings, liver sausages, chaps and pieces of meat, all boiled together in a big copper cauldron, give a strong and tasty soup called 'ovarka'.

Maminka was given the worst part of the work to do - washing and scraping the intestines which are used for the skins of the liver sausages, black puddings and smoked sausages. She had to do it outside in the yard in the hard frost, paddling in icy cold water.

After two days she came home with a hamper containing 2 litres of soup in a can, 2 litres of lard, a piece of the chaps (which Tatinek liked especially), and two liver sausages and two black puddings for each of us. As well as these goodies she also acquired a nasty inflammation of the bladder and tonsillitis accompanied by a high fever, so in the middle of the night Stana had to run for Doctor Fiala who lanced poor suffocating Maminka's tonsils. Tatinek and Stana had to help the doctor during this operation - one was shining a light into Maminka's throat with an electric torch (the paraffin lamp did not give enough light) and the other was catching in a saucer the blood and pus pouring from Maminka's mouth. I ran out into the kitchen.

Maminka had never before been so ill. She stayed in bed nearly two weeks, and the doctor had to open one of the tonsils once more. The pig killing hamper had been very dearly paid for, and poor Maminka could not taste anything of it - except for the lard which lasted us for cooking for several months. When she finally left her bed she was as thin and pale as a shadow.

At the beginning of February I brought home my half term report from school. Never before had I had such poor marks. There were only two '1''s there - for painting and for technical drawing. For German Language, to which I had a complete aversion, I had a '4'! At this time school results were marked out of 5, 5 being the lowest. I was very depressed. People were calling us 'the runaways' and sometimes we even had to hear remarks that we should have stayed where we were. At school my schoolfellows were laughing at my non-Slovak accent. Even for singing I had a '2' - my voice was changing and I could hardly talk, never mind sing! Nor were things completely right at home. Tatinek was unhappy in his new job, which he hated, and I understood from occasional allusions that he was pursued there by the pretty, sexy wife of the invalid Director of the school. Our poor lodgings didn't help the situation either, he missed his evening relaxation with a glass of wine, he became irritable and peevish, and often in the evenings went to the local pub where he fell in with a group of regulars. His salary, lower than it had been in Znojmo, was insufficient, the cost of goods was rising rapidly, and it was often necessary to draw money from our savings. I was going through all the discomforts of puberty, and with the over-sensitivity which accompanied them I felt all the changes twice as painfully.

On the first day of our second term at school, there came to our class a new classmate, the daughter of the Director of the school. Her name was Zorka, and her family had just moved to Straznice from Brno. She was smallish with a slightly olive complexion, longish dark hair and beautiful almost black eyes. There was something of the mystery of the orient about her, and she had a melodic and gentle voice. My first glance at her awoke in me the picture of my dream girl, Mona, from Curwood's 'Men of Brave Hearts'.

Next day, during the main break, a few boys stayed in

the classroom. In the middle of the group was Ricica -'The Shrimp'. He was talking as an 'expert' about Zorka; he said that all girls in Brno are 'light'. I was surprised that the other boys listened to him. For sure they had not read Curwood's book about Mona and didn't know that 'a man must always stand up for a woman!'. And so I fell foul of 'The Shrimp' myself. I told him that he knew nothing at all about Zorka and therefore he should not talk about her in such a manner. 'The Shrimp' replied rudely to me, I pushed him and a fight developed, interrupted only by the ringing of the bell for the end of break, so neither of us won or lost, but at least I had the satisfaction that I had done all that I could in the circumstances. It was the first, and last, time I fought with anybody other than Stana. Even our brotherly skirmishes were diminishing!

Zorka had for me through all the following school years a captivating magic, only my feelings found no response. She enchanted even older boys who wooed her and were certainly more successful than I, but she was kind to me - after all, she was so nice that everybody had to like her.

Uncle Slavek offered, through Tatinek, to negotiate the purchase of a cheap bicycle made at some small agricultural factory. Having parted with the Reichl's small bike in Znojmo I was longing for one of my own, so Tatinek ordered it for me for my fifteenth birthday. This one was green and cost only 300 crowns, when the usual cost of a plain, ordinary bicycle was 1,000 - 1,200 crowns, but I was very happy with it. I stood it in the stable and looked forward to the Spring - hoping that I would grow a little more so that I could reach the pedals from the saddle. There were not many chrome parts on the bike, but those there were started to rust in a very short time, so Tatinek sent it back to the factory with a list of all its faults. After some weeks it was returned with better chrome and the faults repaired. It turned out to be the best bicycle which I ever had.

Whilst we were still in Znojmo we had ordered from 'our' textile firm, Skoda, quite a quantity of material, but as a result of the political situation our order had not been sent to us. After settling in Straznice we urged the despatch of the goods, and at last a large parcel was delivered to us. There was much more in it than we had ordered. The firm was selling their wares cheaply so that they would not fall into German hands and to their good customers they added, with a very modest bill, more things than had been paid for. To us they even added two free items, a big bath towel and a large silk tablecloth. We happily paid the extra amount, and had a reserve of firstclass textiles for many years. Amongst the bed linen, towels, cloths, handkerchiefs and lengths of cotton was some extra fine English men's suiting. This parcel arrived just in the nick of time; our worst apprehensions now changed to reality ...

15th March was a dark, grey day and the sky was weeping with snow and rain. The Czechoslovak tragedy reached its climax. Even the crippled and diminished

Republic came to an end. It was not sufficient for Hitler to have torn away our borderlands; he now occupied the rest of Bohemia and Moravia and made of them the so-called 'Protectorate'. Slovakia broke away and proclaimed herself as the independent Slovakian State. After 300 years of subjection by the Hapsburgs our independent Republic lasted only 20 years and 6 months. Perhaps it now became clear to the western powers, France and especially England, that peace in Europe was secured for only a very short time by giving our so-called 'Sudetenland' to the Nazis, that it had been only an overture to the war which would afflict even those to whom we had unsuccessfully been praying for help.

By creating the 'Protectorate' there fell into Hitler's lap not only our arsenal of weapons, aircraft and tanks which were of a high technical standard (the Czech Bren gun was the best in the world of its type), but with the occupation of Plzen (Pilsen) he took possession of the largest central European armaments factory, Skoda, making heavy weapons, especially guns, and light, fast tanks which formed the basis of his later 'Blitzkrieg' in western Europe.

Just before the occupation the Czech government under President Benes went into exile in England, followed by many Czechs including pilots who were later fighting in the Battle of Britain. Dr Emil Hacha, though already old and ill was appointed the new puppet President of the Protectorate.

The Germans started their 'protecting' occupation by

shooting at the protesting university students, and one of them, Jan Opletal, was killed. They then immediately closed all Czech universities, technical colleges and high schools and arrested many professors, writers, artists and intellectuals.

German soldiers were buying quantities of goods in bulk from Czech shops, sending full boxes of food and other goods back to Germany where there was a great shortage of these things. The unrealistic rate of 1 DM for 10 crowns was fixed for the worthless mark, and so in a short time the shops were almost empty and the prices of any remaining goods grew daily. Many shopkeepers and speculators had their pockets full of marks for which it was possible to buy less and less.

Soon after the occupation, before the main school holiday, we had to tear out from our atlases all the maps which showed Czechoslovakia, and in our geography books all references to England and France we had to black out with indian ink or glue over with a clean piece of paper. Even in our physics books we must black out the words 'England' or 'English'. Then came the purging of the school library , and that continued even after the holiday. The school librarian, Professor Huska, liked Stana so much that he got him to help with the re-organisation of the library. All books by French, English, American and Russian writers were discarded and sent to be burnt. From hundreds of these books Stana managed to smuggle home, and so save, only two - Charles Dickens's 'A Christmas Carol' and a book of short stories by Edgar Allan Poe. Both the books made a deep impression on me - they were such a different genre of literature.

By destroying books, the Germans were following in the tradition of the Vandals - they were ruthlessly liquidating everything that was contrary to their 'Superculture'.

Even the radio receivers in each household were expertly 'castrated'- that is to say, from them were removed the parts which made it possible to listen to short wave programmes. On all receivers had to be fixed a card on which was printed 'REMEMBER that listening to a foreign programme will be punished by imprisonment or death'. But we could not listen to our radio anyway; we had no electricity in our home.

A total blackout was decreed. At night all the streets were without lighting, and there had to be heavy black curtains on all windows so that the light from the houses could not be seen from outside.

The streets were patrolled by German soldiers; now we were prisoners in our own country.

When Spring came, in our two hour drawing lesson, we went to the castle park, everybody choosing his own motif, and we were drawing with pencil what we saw, without any advice or help. I chose a half decayed tree, and the drawing was so successful that it was exhibited in the school. I had never before drawn from nature. I had my own sketchbooks in which, for many years, I had been copying pictures for my own pleasure from books and magazines, but this was the first time I had drawn outdoors. My success in school and the new view of nature encouraged me so that I used from time to time to go into the park even outside school lessons to draw something.

During the second half of the school year I found that I was accepted by the other members of my class, and even became part of a small, select group with whom I went on cycling expeditions around the countryside near Straznice. Of course Zorka was also amongst our group, which later on became called 'The Strong Seven'. Sometimes we were joined by an excellent violinist, Slavek Volavy, two years older than we were, who was so enchanted by Slovak traditional music and songs that, spending much more time on music than on his studies, he failed his exams and had to repeat one year. Later on he formed his own Slovak band, graduated from the conservatory of music after the war, became a Doctor of Music and was a well known personality. He was the chief initiator and co-founder of the national, and later international, Festival of Folk Music and Song in Straznice. He was an extremely sensitive boy and I liked him for his gentleness, even though he sometimes tried to cover it 'with a rough coat'.

We used to sing with Slavek on our wanderings. He knew hundreds of Slovak songs, and the singing took such a hold of us that even in school we filled the breaks between lessons with song. We became known as the 'singing class', and we continued with this habit right through the next four years to the end of our studies.

At the end of the school year we were given

psychological tests to decide who should finish with their studies and who should continue. Some professor came from Brno. He gave each of us a folder of numbered sheets of paper with different problems on each, each one to be solved within a fixed time. We should link together the numbered points and so complete a simple picture, count the numbers of different sizes of interwoven triangles, note the differences between two apparently similar pictures, mark the similarities in two differing pictures, in a printed text underline similar words or letters, and in a column of numbers underline the even numbers or those in which the number 5 appeared, etc. There were about 30 tests in all and we were busy with them for the whole day. For me it was just like a child's game; I had the ability to see the required details or numbers as if they were standing before my eyes without the need to search for them, tediously line by line, so in half a minute I solved things for which others needed five minutes (no wonder that today solving crosswords and puzzles is one of my hobbies!). So, most of the time I sat with folded arms, looking out of the window. The professor asked me several times why I was not working, and when I told him each time that I had finished he came to see and, without speaking, returned once more to his desk. For the last hour of the examination we should write anything we liked - a story from our life, our future plans or something like that - and then the folders, marked with our names, were collected from us.

About two weeks later our classmaster Prof. Zurek told us that he had received the results of the tests. Letters would be sent to the parents of those students who had not achieved the necessary number of marks, but that he wanted only to mention the names of three pupils who had shown exceptional intelligence - Jakubicek, Micek and - surprisingly - Misa. The results of the tests clearly did not correspond to my normal school marks - therefore the 'surprisingly'.

At the end of the school year Stana brought home his school report 'with honour', and our parents gave him a beautiful bicycle which was exactly four times as expensive as mine had been. But he deserved it. The last time he had had a report 'with honour' had been in his first year in the gymnasium when his reward had been a camera.

I again had '4' for German language, and was better in physics and chemistry for which in both subjects I had '1's.

By the time of the main school holiday, though it was still too big for me I was already using my bicycle but without it's saddle because I still couldn't reach the pedals. Using a piece of a potato sack I improvised a small cushion which I fixed with a piece of string onto the end of the bar. It was not the most comfortable of saddles, but cycling was so much better than running.

Our immediate neighbours were the Gajdas. A short way out of Straznice they had an apple orchard, and because there was already by then a shortage of fruits, Mr Gajda asked me to guard the orchard.

At one end of the orchard was a hut, and a bit further on, beyond the track which ran beside the field, there stretched Bata's transport canal. At the time it was half empty, and the level of the water in it was still slowly dropping because they were repairing the lock near the weir on the River Morava which supplied the canal with water. In a few days the water reached only to my knees, and the lower it became, the warmer it got. Each day I splashed about in it several times, and I noticed the narrow grooves left behind by the slow moving fresh water mussels. I saw, too, the small perch, how they moved their translucent yellow pectoral fins, how they relaxed in the footprints I had made the previous day on the soft bottom of the canal, and I enjoyed all the pleasures which the water gave me.

Like every true boy, I had my rubber catapult with me, the one which I had made back in Znojmo, wearing it stuck into the belt of my shorts. In my back pocket was my ammunition of a few cubes of lead, also from those I had cast whilst in Znojmo. I never shot anything, except on that morning.

As I did every morning, I left the shed at first light, brushing from myself the pieces of straw which clung to me from the two bundles on which I had been sleeping. I listened to the calling of the pheasants whilst I warmed my coffee on a small fire in front of the shed. Stana would bring my lunch to me on his bicycle. Later Tatinek would bring my supper, and breakfast for the following morning. After breakfast I picked up the windfall apples and went to look at the canal to see how much the water had dropped again. I washed there and cleaned my teeth; by then the sun had risen.

I walked beside the canal for about an hour, watching the little perch again, when all at once I saw, some way away near the opposite edge of the water something flashing white, and I heard a splash. Against the sun which was still low in the sky I could not really see what it was there, and when the water quietened again I almost lost interest in it. But then I thought that I would like to see what had been the reason. If it was a duck struggling with a mussel it certainly could not vanish! So I went down to the water and was wading to where I had seen the splash. After about 150 steps the water was once again frothing. It was near the edge where, only a hand's span under the water, was a flat sandy bottom, and I could already see what it was - a huge perch! He just managed to swim from the shallow to deeper water. With one hand I reached for my catapult, with the other a lead cube from my pocket and - bang! in the water! The perch thrashed out to one side, but I had already taken aim at him again just under his head. I shot, the water splashed, the fish jumped into the air, fell back and stayed just under the water, belly uppermost. Only when I had picked up the dead fish and was carrying it across the canal did I feel how excited I was and how my knees were shaking. Walking through the water I noticed, on my right, near the bottom, some other movement. It was again a perch, and a big one too. I hurried to get my catch to the shed, hiding it under the straw, and came back to the canal. The perch was still there, and he ended with only one shot from me, straight into the top of his head.

I did not look for any more fish. I tried to pack my catch in my bread bag, but could squeeze in it only one of the perch. I hid the smaller one under the straw again, locked the shed, put the strap of the bag with my fish over my shoulder and pedalled home as fast as I could, arriving home nearly breathless. I didn't say too much. I put the fish on the table and went back for the second one. This time I was followed by Stana who would undertake the guarding of the orchard for me while I was absent. When I came home with the second perch, Maminka told me that the first one weighed 1.20 kg. I straight away weighed the second, he lacked only 50 gms to weigh a full kilo. I gutted them and stripped off the skins because it was impossible to scrape away the scales.

Next day, 20.7.1939, Tatinek got a fishing licence for me from the local fishing club. At last!! It was my first real fishing licence, and it meant that I could be sitting with my rod by the water without fear.

If earlier I had been searching my surroundings as well as guarding the orchard, now I was guarding the orchard as an adjunct to fishing. I cut two good rods from a young mountain ash in the castle park, I plaited my fishing line from strong button thread, I bought the hooks, and I *really* started to fish.

Behind the further end of the orchard were two blind arms of the main river of the country, the Morava, called Vesky and Prachar's Lagoon. They were hidden places where you could find only roe deer, pheasants, and perhaps the occasional fisherman - a perfect fishing paradise. I started in Vesky, which ended at the river wall that, following the flow of the river, should hold the spring and autumn spates of water. In approximately the last third of the arm I found a good place from which to fish. It was a level spot just above the water. At my back a steep bank of bushes hid the place which was as flat as a table and at one end dropping at a right angle down to the water's edge where there grew wild irises and reeds. When I was sitting down I was almost completely hidden, even from across the water.

I was soon at home on this spot. I stuck y-shaped twigs, which I had cut from the alders growing nearby, into the earth in front of me and on them laid my two ash rods and my old one of bamboo which I still had from Znojmo.

By 5 o'clock in the morning I was already squatting on 'my' spot. The fish started to bite about half an hour later when everything was quiet again. It was very deep there, one metre from the bank the hook dropped into a pool about 2 metres deep. The bottom was full of dead twigs and branches; on previous days I had pulled out many of them and broken more than one hook on them until I had learned where were the clear and safe places.

The big advantage of my place was that it was not necessary to cast the line, I had only to drop it into the water just a few feet from the land. If only, though, those mosquitoes were not there! I stretched the trousers of my track suit over my feet, I wore old leather gloves or drew my sleeves over my hands, and on my head I stuck a large paper bag with holes only for my eyes and mouth. There were complete clouds of mosquitoes, so that they looked like a moving veil of fog against the sky. I smoked a pipe - or rather, I was not actually smoking but just making smoke so that they would be driven away from me a little. It was a necessity. Even though my tongue was already as rough as a grater I filled my pipe again and again with tobacco, but the mosquitoes were still biting most painfully through my track suit, some of them flying into the paper bag on my head and the especially hungry and impertinent ones even biting me on my lip in spite of the smoke from my pipe.

However when the float on one of my lines moves I immediately forget the mosquitoes. It is the ash rod on the right - knock, knock, and then nothing. After a few seconds it jerks again and moves three inches further out, a little to one side, swings, bobs on the water and is slowly drawn under the surface. I strike and play the fish towards the land. Easy, easy, don't struggle - you are mine already! A good tench.

I am catching mostly tench here, with occasionally some smaller perch or rudd. Even the tench are not big, only up to 1lb in weight.

One is biting again, this time on the bamboo rod. It seems that today I might catch at least half a dozen. I had been fishing on this spot for more than a week already and never gone home without fish. Two days before I had caught even eight of them.

Whirr... something startles me! In front of my nose

there flashes a flying blue and red spark - one of the pair of kingfishers which usually sit on a branch of the alder growing on my left, from which they can see into the water. It settles once again on the same spot, but where is the second? I haven't seen him today as yet. Ah! - see he is coming already - straight onto my bamboo rod. Is it possible that he hasn't seen me? It seems so. I had already stopped smoking when the first tench started to bite, and I am sitting very quietly. I am astonished, though, that he is not alarmed by the white paper bag on my head. And now something is biting on the bamboo rod, but I mustn't move! The beauty with his long beak and short tail really cannot have seen me, otherwise he would not behave so rashly. He stretches his right wing and is nibbling under it with his beak - I can see each feather.

Suddenly the rod jerks, the kingfisher whirrs away, and something is pumping at the rod. The line is stretched to the deeper water. That is what happens when I am watching a kingfisher instead of my float! I am already holding the rod. It must be something larger, for no previous fish has been struggling so much with me. And it would be that on this rod I have the thin line. Now it snags somewhere down below on a sunken branch. What shall I do with it? If I had a reel the fish could pull out more of the line, which is already so stretched that in desperation I have had to lay the rod on the water. The tip sinks a little, the thicker end pumping up and down on the surface of the water, but then the whole rod is floating away again to the middle of the water.

I pull off my paper hood, my track suit, shirt and pants and in seconds am covered with biting mosquitoes. After slipping into the water without disturbing it too much I swim to the rod. When I am already near, it turns in another direction and floats away. Now it has stopped. Soon I am up to it, catch the tip and take the line so I can feel the movement of the fish and even manage to pull in some of the line, but when the fish responds harder I let some of it go between my fingers again. It is terribly difficult to tread water and at the same time try to get near the bank whilst leading the fish with the rod, but the fish is already tired. When at last, after what seems to be an endless length of time I feel the bottom under my feet, I try to pull the line with the fish towards me. At last I touch him, but startle him so much that he struggles violently and I must release the line once again. It is his last effort to escape. After that it is easy to pull him to me, I catch him firmly by the gills, holding him with all my power. It is a tench, and I know very well already how slippery is a tench's body. What a beauty! He must weigh nearly 1 kilo.

Is it possible that I went so far in hunting him? How long have I been in the water? I feel how stiff I am . The rod in one hand, in the other the fish, I wade to the bank, sinking up to my ankles in the silt, but at last I back on dry land and can run to my fishing place. Even whilst I am running the mosquitoes are attacking me, and I must pass through a thicket of nettles which reach over my head. Finally I am there. I must finish for this morning so I pull on my pants and trousers even over my muddy feet and dress hurriedly in my shirt and anorak. Speedily I pack my rods, stuff my tobacco and pipe - which is already cold - into my pocket, put both the fish into my fishing bag, laying them on the paper hat which I had damaged during my quick strip, pull on my tennis shoes - I will wash the mud from them in the canal. And now hurry, hurry from here! My neck is already full of bites, my lip is nicely swollen and my wrists are as if on fire.

In the sunshine it is already a bit better. The itching has not stopped at all, but mosquitoes are no longer biting me, they stay in the shade, and at last I feel warmer too. The water was not very warm.

I had never before seen such clouds of mosquitoes, and I have never again suffered so badly from their bites as I did by those blind arms of Morava. No more than twenty seconds were necessary for my hands to be completely covered with thirsty mosquitoes and feeling worse than if I had been whipping myself with a bunch of nettles. The itching and burning increased so that in the night it was intolerable. Next morning I would leave my bed sleepy and tired, the skin on the worst places scratched to blood and swollen as if I had been stung by bees. Even my eyelids were so swollen that I could hardly see and I had a fever so that I felt really ill. But that did not stop me from fishing, either that year or in later years, in which my body adapted to the mosquitoes so that in the end I hardly noticed them and I had to drive away only the most intrusive. And, surprisingly, the places where they bit swelled less and less, until in the end they did not swell at all, nor did they itch.

Before I reached this immunity I tried many recommended anti-mosquito preparations, all more or less repulsive. I tried turpentine, paraffin, engine oil, onion, garlic, eau de Cologne, liquids and creams from the chemist, but nothing helped. I was unpleasantly perfumed only for human noses, the mosquitoes bit as before. The only efficient protection was to stop them reaching my skin by dressing well. In the summer heat, when one was hot even in swimming pants only, it was not at all comfortable and the mosquitoes were able to bite even through a double layer of track suit! I often used to watch them, how they would search and try to find a possible place through which to poke their probosces, but I also saw that they usually found it. And then would start the all too well known itching, the mosquito's abdomen filling and swelling and becoming dark red until it was as shiny as a miniature bottle of burgundy.

In a few weeks there was an end to the peace of my first successful fishing-ground. People came from Vnorovy with nets shaped like sacks and plundered the water without mercy. They were taking everything - tench, perch, rudd, bream, chub, pike and even the mussels for their ducks. Soon I stopped fishing there. I caught not even one small fish. The beautiful pike who each morning had been hunting about 10m from my spot vanished, as did dozens of other fish, mostly chub, which had been standing without moving during the time of the midday heat, just below the surface under the alders. The morning and evening splashing of hunting pikes ceased, not one was left in the water. And how many there had been! Some evenings, during the half hour when the pike were feeding, the water was never free of their splashing! It was a pity that at that time I hadn't yet known how to catch a pike myself!

Behind Bata's canal was a ditch which drained the meadows and was carried under the canal through a concrete 'syphon' to a deep basin, also of concrete and about 2.5 x4m in size, out of which the water flowed along another ditch to a second blind arm of the Morava.

When I first found the basin, I heard only a few splashes and saw that the surface of the water was disturbed. I stopped there to see what could have caused them. Three or four toads soon rose to the top and, with outstretched legs, continued with their sunbathing in the warm water. I lay on the ground so that I could see from above if there was anything more in the water. After a while there slowly rose from the depths several fishes - half a dozen small chub, which took up their positions in the shallow running water at the start of the ditch, a school of tiny bleaks which stayed in one corner of the basin, and finally there slowly emerged a small pike, weighing about 1 lb. The bleaks swam a safe distance away from him. The pike had a marbled, olive green back, big eyes turning jerkily towards the small fish, and I could see even the movement of his translucent pectoral fins and the flexing of his tail as the hunter changed his position.

Around the reeds growing at the start of the ditch flew a dragonfly and, a little further on, a few azure damselflies. The dragonfly had its own observation post on top of a piece of a dead branch which stuck out from the side of the ditch in front of the reeds. He could see well from there and was waiting for some of the small flies dancing above the water. From there he shot out like an arrow, attacking his prey with an audible rustling of his wings and flying back with his catch to the branch where he ate it - he left only the wings which, circling in the air, fell onto the water below.

Once something flew round my head, so near that I could hear the rustling of the wings which was gentler than that of the dragonfly. It was some larger insect, and I thought that I noticed, even when it was flying, the pair of front legs half closed like a penknife. The insect fell into the vegetation at the start of the ditch and, because I had read that in South Moravia one could sometimes find the rare praying mantis, I stopped with my observation of the fishes and climbed with rapidly beating heart down to the water's edge to start to look for it. And I was lucky enough to find it! Its grasping forelegs clearly showed the relationship with the mantis family, but the slimmer, brown body reminded me more of the stick insects. I ran with my catch to the shed in the orchard where I made a cornet out of a piece of newspaper in which I enclosed my 'mantis', and went home on my bicycle so that I could take advice from Brehm's 'Life of Animals', but I found neither picture nor description of my catch in the book. I put the insect in a glass terrarium which I had made from an old electric accumulator, putting in some flies as food.

Next day my 'mantis' was dead. She was noticeably much slimmer, and in the terrarium was a small, dark, grooved case which clearly held eggs, which the insect had layed. I was sorry that she had not been able to lay her eggs in the wild, and so that the eggs were not wasted I packed them with the dead insect and sent it with a letter to the Moravian Museum in Brno, hoping that there they would be able to breed the larvae and adult imagos from the eggs and that they would tell me the exact name of the insect. I waited a long time for their reply, and it was only when I had written a second time that I learnt that it was a mantis-stick insect, so it was really something between the two, and that the eggs had not hatched, probably because they had dried too much.

After the corn harvest our farmer neighbour, Mr Gajda, sold us a sack of wheat and a sack of rye - the wheat for cakes and dumplings and the rye for bread. Because under the rationing system introduced by the Germans it was possible to buy only a very limited quantity of food, scarcely sufficient to cover the most basic necessities, it was a very welcome addition to our fare. Of course, selling us the corn which was designated for State supplies so that the Nazi forces could be fed, was illegal, as was the milling of the corn for flour, and such transactions were strictly punishable. The mill's production was controlled by German officers, but somehow our sacks slipped unnoticed into the mill and out again too. The miller, Pruzek, the father of my classmate, Jarin, helped people without thought for himself whenever it was possible to do so.

We were buying potatoes from the Gajdas too. We really badly needed a bit of extra food. I had at last started to grow, and in less than one year I was so lanky that I was the tallest in our family, and also the leanest. I was now 175 cms tall and weighed only 52 kgs; I was permanently hungry. Sometimes I had even to leave my bed in the night and cut myself a slice of bread to still the pangs in my stomach.

The school holidays ended. Because of my poor results in German, our class master recommended that I should take private lessons. The teacher lived in a small cottage on the outskirts of the town, and she introduced me on my first visit to her father and sister. They were Jews. The father, who had a small shop for scrap metals and rabbit skins, was wearing a black kaftan, a full white beard and, on his head, a small embroidered velvet cap. The daughters were unmarried and not very beautiful, but they both had such large, dark, sad eyes. All three of them had, as commanded by the Germans, a yellow Star of David sewn to their chest.

I was learning in a small room with heavy curtains of red velvet on the window. It was quiet there, everything was meticulously tidy, neatly arranged books and little embroidered covers everywhere where it was possible to put them. Against a side wall was a black piano.

My teacher had a quiet, melodic voice which freed me

from my first nervousness and insecurity. Her teaching was quite different to that in school. We were talking in German about my interests, about nature and about daily things. After the lesson a tray was brought in by her sister, as quietly as if by a little mouse, with home made biscuits and a pot of hot cocoa which she left with only a smile and a wish for a 'good appetite'.

I had lessons twice a week, and soon I was looking forward to them. The little room was an island of peace, my teacher was goodness and kindness personified, and I discovered an unusual charm behind those sad eyes.

About a month later my teacher told me that we must say 'goodbye' because in two days' time they would be moved to the concentration camp at Treblinka in Poland. She told me then that they were not rich, but that she would like to give me the family silver cutlery and a few pieces of jewellery and gold coins. I should ask at home if my parents would agree to the idea.

My parents thought that I could not accept such a gift and so I went to say so to her. The teacher showed some sadness after my news. She told me that she understood but that she knew the things would have been in good hands. After that she caressed me on my cheek and quickly went away with tears in her eyes.

Certainly she died in one of the Nazi's elimination camps, as did 6 million other Jews, including 1½ million small children, and the family relics were stolen by the Germans. Only later did I understand through what the poor, good soul must have passed before she was liberated by death. The shocking news at the end of the war which brought to light the atrocities perpetrated in the elimination camps stopped being mere statistics when they affected somebody with whom we had accepted hospitality, been sitting at one table, and taking from the same pot and dish.

At this same time Maminka's brother, Uncle Jan, was arrested. It was he who played the small concertina at home and who had guinea-pigs in his rabbit hutches. The reason for his arrest was his involvement in the union of building workers, being a carpenter. The Nazis held that any organisation other than their own was dangerous to them. They were hunting especially for communists and members of unions, the latter being the nearest to communists. My uncle was imprisoned for all the six years, and returned home only after the war.

Even from Romanov, a small village of settled gypsies on the edge of Straznice, where were the blacksmith, basket maker, cartwright and other craftsmen, all the inhabitants were moved to a concentration camp and their cottages were destroyed and razed to the ground. The gypsies met the same fate as the Jews - in the gas chambers.

The Nazis' hatred of the 'unclean' Jews was such that all citizens must give the German authorities an official extract from their parish register of births right back to the fourth generation so that it was certain that in his ancestry was not one drop of Jewish blood. If he had 'contaminated' blood Tatinek would not have been able to stay in his office and Stana and I would not be allowed to continue with our studies.

Whilst my school results stagnated on a not very high level, Stana's improved considerably and, possibly through his increased self-confidence as a result of this improvement, our mutual respect began to change, our continual struggles and skirmishes ceased.

Perhaps my school marks would have been a bit better if I had spent more time in studying. But - who knows?, because the subjects in which I was interested I remembered well from the lessons we were given in school without the need for further studying and, in contrast, any subject in which I had no interest I did not remember at all no matter how hard I tried to learn it at home, and anyway I had so many other interests...!

Somebody in our street gave us a tabby kitten. It was very sweet, with large blue eyes and a short little nose. Zolina was at this time four years old and had not previously met a cat in her own home, so when she first sniffed at Minka the hackles rose on her back, but after our warning she left the kitten in peace and soon they became good friends, in time even playing together.

Once when Zolina was eating bread and milk from her bowl Minka went straight up to her, between her front legs, and in a few moments there was the sound of them both eating together. When the bowl was empty the two of them started to lick the last drops of milk from each other's whiskers.

Bread and milk formed the basic diet of both the dog and the cat, but Minka liked best of all the fresh little fish which I brought her from my fishing trips. She used to growl whilst she was eating them, and she stopped only when she had finished the very last fish. Usually she was so impatient that she climbed up my leg right to my shoulder so that I would give her her delicacy and, because of the fish, we were especially close one to the other.

One evening Mrs Zabelka came to visit us and when she was leaving, still standing in the half open street door to say a few words, Minka took advantage of the situation and slipped out to the street. I immediately went to catch her, but she vanished in the darkness. I went home for a torch and was searching and calling for her until late into the night, but the kitten was gone and never came back. We were all sad about it, including Zolina, who had adopted the kitten already as her puppy, and I missed so much Minka's walking around me, miaowing and asking for her fish each time that I came back from the water.

Towards the end of the summer a wild turtle dove arrived at our house. She sat on the wooden fence and, when I came towards her slowly with outstretched arm and soothing words, she moved only a few small steps to one side, but didn't fly away. After a few minutes she let me stroke her throat, and finally let me catch her. She was so beautiful with the dark ring round her neck, pink legs and perfectly smooth plumage. She soon became accustomed to me. I made a cage for her out of a wooden box and a piece of wire netting, but during the day I used to let her fly free in the room . When I was writing my school homework at the table she used to sit on my shoulder, stroking her head against my cheek and chin and gently nibbling the moving end of my pen with her beak.

Much less time was needed for a young tawny owl which was given to me from the nearby village. I kept him in the stable. He could not fly yet and he was the complete opposite to the dove, always dishevelled, sleepy and surly, but he had a very nice head and huge yellow eyes. I fed him with pieces of meat which he gulped down greedily, but after a few days I found him lying dead. Only much later did I learn that owls need to swallow the small bones and fur of their prey for their digestive systems to function properly.

Then Fabre's book 'The Life of the Spider' inspired me with the idea of breeding spiders. For this I used the glass container in which I had earlier had my 'mantis'. I put in it some larger pieces of pine tree bark under which the spiders could hide, and a few branches on which they could spin their webs. I covered the open part of my 'vivarium' with a piece of cardboard glued to the rim, and in the cardboard I cut a small easily closed slot through which to feed the spiders with flies.

I collected the spiders at night, using a small electric torch and catching them in a glass. They came from the crevices in an old wooden fence, and I took mostly the largest, the garden cross spiders, but other smaller ones as well.

From Fabre's book I learned that spiders' eyes reflect the light in a similar way to cats' eyes. And really, now I could see it was so, and was astonished at these minute emeralds, sapphires and rubies which shone on their heads as little bulbs when the direction of the light from my torch was right.

I fed them with living flies, and once I put a wasp into the vivarium. It immediately stuck to a web, and alerted by the movement of the lines, a large garden cross spider at once attacked the wasp. The wasp was much stronger than an ordinary fly and tore the lines of the web, nearly managing to escape, but the spider dashed to it, turned her abdomen towards it and glued a dense bunch of threads onto the wasp whilst revolving it with her legs, covering the prey with a bandage of the web extruded from the spinnerets at the end of her abdomen. The wasp struggled, trying to reach the spider with her sting which she poked through the emeshing threads and biting a hole through them. The spider kept a safe distance from the sting, biting the wasp several times while covering it again with more threads, and in the end was the winner. For me it was a wonderful mystery - how did the spider know about the danger of being stung by a wasp? Her evident respect for it could never have been gained through experience because a spider could not possibly survive the sting of a wasp.

The purgatory of our emergency lodging finished at last, and in the Autumn we moved into another cottage. It was not far away, in the same street called 'Little

Cottages'. Once again it was only a kitchen and one room, but the building was dry and had electricity installed. The entrance to the cottage was protected by a porch built of bricks and with a large window, where we could keep our bicycles and other things and my dove had her cage there too. With this move I thankfully escaped from sleeping in the damp stone 'tomb' in the dark kitchen-dungeon.

We increased the furnishing of our new kitchen with the bench on which we had been sitting in the lorry during our removal from Znojmo and which until now had been in Pavlovice. The bench had an upholstered back, and the surface on which we sat was of three hard pillows which, at night made broader by the addition of chairs, made quite a good 'bed' on which I was sleeping. Stana slept on the couch in our parents' bedroom. Our lavatory was once again just a wooden hut out on the yard. Each Saturday we bathed ourselves in a light metal tub, which we had bought just after moving to Straznice, and which we brought in each time from the porch to our kitchen.

At school we were taught history by Professor Janicek. He had previously been teaching in Slovakia but after the breaking away of Slovakia, where the nationalist leader Hlinka had for several years been running an anti-Czech campaign, the Czechs there - as 'unwanted elements' - must leave the country. And so he was afflicted with a similar fate as we, even though his wife was Slovakian not Czech. I liked him, he was so gentle and sensitive. I was only sorry that in my exams I could not produce better results for him. I still struggled with history.

In the first term of the fifth class he was lecturing to us about styles of classical architecture. At last - here was something really interesting! As much as I could not digest political history, I was totally absorbed by the cultural history. It was something with a shape which I could imagine - and for my tests I had the best mark - a '1'! Even in the following lectures about Philip of Macedonia and Alexander the Great, when we were told about new technical discoveries and so on, I was again successful in my marks, so that for the first time since the first class of the gymnasium I brought home a certificate for history with the mark '1'. Sadly, though, my glory did not last too long. In the second term it was once again a '3'!

My free time was now confined to weekends, when I tried fishing in Bata's canal, which was once again full of water and from where I was bringing home small perch and rudd. I cleaned them and took off the skins from the perch, and Tatinek pickled them with onion, mustard seeds, vinegar, salt, crushed peppercorns and allspice which we still had from before the war as they were used for pickling herrings. Pickled herrings were Tatinek's favourite supper, and the small fish which I caught were just as good. Sometimes Tatinek came with me to the water, and so he too started to discover the magic of fishing.

I only wished I could catch something bigger, but after the emptying of the canal in summer no bigger fish were left. I had been lucky when I shot those two perch. What would happen when I tried somewhere else - perhaps in Prachar's pool?

This pool was about 20 metres in diameter, which lay as a lagoon on one arm of the Morava river and originally had been joined to the place where I had been catching the good tench whilst I was guarding the apple orchard in the summer. In the first part the water stood without any movement. The drainage ditch ran into the second part so there there was a slight current. In summer the left bank of the pool rose above the water as a steep wall about 3 metres high. The river bed changed direction at this point to run at a right angle, and the spates of water from the melting snow in the spring and the rains in autumn regularly undermined the bank. At those times the river bed was full to the top and often flooded over the surrounding areas.

It was possible to ride my bicycle almost to the water's edge, firstly on the Straznice to Bzenec road and thence to the protecting wall beside the forest, which was full of bushes and holes gouged out by the wild waters in which were breeding clouds of mosquitoes. From the wall, however, it was necessary to walk beside my bicycle through a meadow and an old orchard.

In summer, when the water was low, I had been fishing there a few times but had caught nothing bigger then a few small perch and some rudd. On the opposite side of the lagoon I frequently saw a good pike hunting, but he was safe from me there because he was too far away for my tackle.

At that time, inspired by a picture in some old fishing magazine which had come by chance into my hands, I made a pike line. I joined together a few pieces of thinnish string until I had about 20 feet, near the end I put on a cork from a demijohn, and I finished the line with a thin doubled brass wire into which I fitted a double fishing hook. I wound the line onto a short stick and put it into a fishing bag. So far I had had no chance to use it.

One Saturday afternoon, after it had rained for nearly two weeks so that I had not been able to fish, the rain turned to drizzle, and I could not stay at home any longer. I started out on my bike to Prachar's pool.

It was easy cycling on the road, but on the protecting wall so much muddy clay stuck on the bicycle's wheels that I had to lift it onto my shoulder and carry it to the pool.

Standing and looking at the murky waters which were moving scarcely a metre below me, I remembered the summer. The water had been more than 2 metres lower then. Even the reeds at the side had vanished now. Once I had caught in my hand in the reeds a minute shrew, no bigger than a maybeetle. He was climbing to the plumes at the top, looking for food such as a beetle or a spider. When I held him in my palm he did not scratch or try to escape even when I opened my palm a little. He crouched there with shining dark spots of eyes and stretching out his long and bristly nose. When I put him back onto one of the reeds it was as if nothing had happened. He rustled there a bit, then ran to the next. I wondered what could have happened to him. Did he drown ..?

I don't like the brown water at all; it looks dead to me and I can't see any movement of even the smallest fish in it, but having come such a long way I unpack my tackle after all.

I am fishing in the slightly quieter water near the bank, but nothing is happening except for the steady and continuous drizzle. I am watching how a drop of water is moving on my bamboo rod, sliding slowly downwards, accelerating for a brief moment, stopping and finally dropping off at the node.

Is that really a bite? The float moves a fraction, jumps up and down under the water. Only large fish are biting with such speed! I strike, but a tiny rudd no bigger than my finger is flying onto the bank. I want to return it to the water, but then I have a better idea. In my bag I have that line for catching pike.

I fix the little fish on the hook and cast towards the middle of the pool, but the current slowly moves the cork back to the bank. After a while I pull the line out of the water and cast it again into the deeper part, but the result is the same. The cork stops scarcely one metre from the land. I leave it where it is and go back to my rods. I put a fresh worm onto each hook. No movement at all. I feel only how a wet chill is settling on me. I get up and walk some way against the current, washing my muddy boots in the soaking wet grass, and after half an hour I come back. If the worms on my hooks are untouched I will pack up and go home.

I look at the one on my bamboo rod; it is untouched. But there is no time after all in which to look at my ash rod! I hear two 'plop's, followed by four more - it is the cork on my pike line! Now it sinks again with another 'plop'. I jump to it, take it in my hands and can feel a good fish on the hook! I pull it carefully towards me, occasionally loosening the line, but at last there is a nice pike below me - only how am I to take it from the water? I have no landing net, the water is about a metre down and the bank is completely vertical. It is impossible to pull the fish straight up onto the bank. The string, which looked quite adequate when dry, is now soaked with water and hairy, and might possibly break with the added weight of the fish as well.

I lie on my stomach, but cannot reach the water with my hand. However, I can see a small ledge just above the level of the water which should be large enough for one foot. Carefully I step onto it; it holds! In one hand I have my line and am clinging to a bunch of grass, with the other I am trying to catch the fish which is still struggling - but at last I am able to throw it onto the land. In that moment of effort I feel the ledge moving under my foot, and I am slipping. I grab the grass with both hands and manage to pull my body upwards on my elbows until I have my chest on the bank.

I am shaking. Is it from the chill, from the excitement of such a catch, or from the realisation of how difficult it would have been to swim in rubber boots and a long coat?

And what would they say to me at home if I came back completely soaked?

I pour the water, which had been up to my knees, out of my boots, and go to look at the pike. It is beautiful, about 3/4 of a metre long, and to this time my biggest fish. I cannot even guess how heavy it is. Perhaps 2 kilos? It is true that in summer by chance I caught a pike with an earth worm on my hook, but that was a complete dwarf compared to today's. What teeth it has!

I knock it on the head and pack my tackle. I try to put the fish into my fishing bag, but it is so big that I have to leave the tail outside.

The drizzle changes to rain. On the river wall I again have to carry my cycle on my shoulder and this warms me well. Only my feet are still cold in my soaking wet boots. But I forget even that. My heart is singing with joy from such a beautiful catch. I cannot stop looking at the tail shaking at each bounce of the bicycle.

The pike weighed 2.5 kgs, and its stomach was full of big earth worms with no trace of a fish.

That same evening I made another pike line and prepared three ordinary lines with hooks. The next day being Sunday, Tatinek came with me too. We cut three twigs from the forest, and I fixed the prepared lines onto them so that we could try on five rods for smaller fish. We caught only one rudd, a little bigger than that of the day before, and a slightly smaller pike on the rudd. I didn't even try to land this pike from the dangerous bank, bringing it instead about ten metres further along where it was easy to catch it in my hand. It weighed 2.3 kgs, and once again was full of earth worms.

1940

Winter - Chub - The dam at Knezdub - Ceramics workshop - Dancing lessons - Fishing with lines - Moving to Bzenec - Pigkilling

The winter of 1940 was really cruel with hard frosts, the rivers were frozen, and masses of snow fell, but even so it ended at last. There was an epidemic of influenza, and I developed pleurisy after it, so Dr Fiala was once more visiting me. When I left my bed I was even thinner than before and had constant pains on the right side of my chest which troubled me for many years after.

In the river Morava the rushing murky waters from the melting snow carried gigantic icefloes over a metre thick. In some places higher up the river the waters broke through the protecting walls, turning the meadows and forest, behind which I had caught the two good pike, into a lake. The ice floating in it knocked against the tree trunks, scraping off the bark, breaking off branches from the bushes and leaving clumps of brown grass stuck on the boles of trees and on any other obstacle which stood in it's way. After a few days the waters dropped again but the icefloes lay in the forest for more than a month afterwards.

I awaited impatiently for the time when it would be warm once again and I would be able to go and fish again.

On 29th March 1940 Tatinek was moved to another

office, at the trialgrounds for vines and vegetables in Bzenec. As before he was employed there as an accountant, but at least he escaped from the previous office and environment where he was so unhappy. At first he travelled there by bus, but with the coming of the warmer weather he bought himself a bicycle too, so then we had three cycles at home.

Bata's canal - in which I had last summer shot the two perch with my catapult - crossed the river Velicka not far beyond the castle park. The right and left sections of the canal were separated from the river by gates, and a two metre high dam in the river below the crossing held the high water for the canal. Below the dam was a deep, concrete basin.

It was the month of May, with swarms of maybeetles. They were even floating on the surface of the river, having fallen there from the trees growing nearby, when I noticed a strange thing. They all vanished under the dam, not one escaped from the basin. I saw how the water there flowed in a big whirlpool moved by the entry of water from the upper part of the river entering the side of the basin through a conduit. I saw something circling around; it was a beetle carried by the current. The beetle stopped in the quieter water in one corner of the basin, where everything relaxed as if taking energy for circumscribing the next circle. The beetle came near to the concrete wall and suddenly the water underneath it boiled. The beetle vanished. I saw only the flash of a golden body.

So - chub were below the dam! When I saw how the first beetle had ended I shook down about ten more from a small tree and threw them into the basin. All of them were eaten by the fishes.

I ran straight home to get my fishing rod. But my angling was not as successful as I had hoped, the line fixed at the tip of the rod was too short. It needed to be sufficiently long for the beetle on my hook to be able to circulate freely with the water, so I decided on my first larger purchase.

The very next day I went on my bicycle to the nearby town of Veseli where I bought the cheapest fishing reel I could, the rings for leading the line, and ten metres of real monofilament fishing line. When I had made the necessary adjustments to my rod I went back to the dam.

And the chub were biting as crazy! In under half an hour my fishing bag was so full that I had to carry the other fish with a string through their gills. They were mostly about half a kilo in weight, three quarters of a kilo was a good one indeed. It was my heaviest catch to that time. I was expecting a lot from angling in the pool, because I saw more and more fish coming through the shallow waters below the basin into its deep waters. Almost every minute one of the fish would jump up the oblique wall of the dam, hang for a second as if stuck to it, and then fall back into the water. The dam was too steep and high for them.

But, it being a fine Saturday afternoon at the time, many people came past, some of them stopping near me to ask me how I was doing. On the Sunday, when I tried again, there was already another angler on my spot above the successful corner, so I crossed the dam to the other side and was fishing from there. I landed some fish again, but it was not so good as it had been the day before. The chub were clearly congregating in the corner where that first maybeetle had vanished. On Monday I could only go to the water after school, but when I arrived there five anglers were already there, so I didn't even unpack my tackle. I went on my cycle to a place higher up, behind the town.

When I had gone to Veseli to buy my reel I had crossed a bridge over the river Velicka, which was canalised below the bridge but untouched above. A small tributary flowed into a pool there, and then the river twisted between shrubs and trees somewhere into the unknown. What about searching through it?

I walked the bicycle upstream on the bank. On my left the river sometimes murmured over stones or fallen branches, in other places it sank quietly deeper. I threw a beetle into the water. It was taken immediately by a big chub. All the same I did not stop there, anticipating that somewhere higher up *my* place would be waiting for me.

So I walked for more than an hour. The river twisted, sometimes forcing me to make a detour of impassable bushes on the bank, and from time to time I would stop to admire a new pool or an old, hollow willow.

I heard more and more clearly the sound of falling water, and soon found a small dam. The side was built of heavy wooden beams and fell straight into the water, finishing near an ancient willow tree which waved to her sister of the same age on the opposite side of the river where the dam rested on the trunk of the tree. The nearer end of the dam and a sluice were joined to the wooden wall.

The highest beam of this little dam rose only about 3/4 of a metre above the foaming, sparkling waterlevel, and from time to time a chub jumped over it. They were swimming against the stream for spawning, just like salmon.

I decided to come again tomorrow to catch some of them. The light was already starting to fail and it was time to go home. From here I only needed to cross a small area of grassland to reach the field track, from which it was just a stone's throw to the main road. The roofs I could see in the distance must be Knezdub. It was true that the village was no nearer to the dam than was Straznice, but I called it 'Knezdub's little dam', after the village, in which I knew had lived one of our greatest painters of folklore, Joza Uprka,

I went back there several times in the next few days. sitting on top of the vertical wall of beams and fishing with two rods. The line of my ash rod I dropped in the deep water below the dam, immediately beneath me; with my bamboo rod and reel I cast under the willow on the opposite bank. I brought home so many fish Maminka started to complain that she had to use too much of our precious lard for frying them, so I sold some of my catch.

On Saturdays Tatinek came to fish with me too. We had started fishing together in the Autumn when I caught that second good pike, and now his original curiosity had changed into a real enthusiasm for fishing. Even today I can see how thrilled he was when he caught his first chub and how his hands were shaking!

We usually fished below the dam, but in the shallowish waters above it we also had good catches using the maybeetles. Later in the month, when the supply of beetles began to diminish, we started to use earthworms. The fish did not bite so well on them as on the beetles but once, just as the sun began to set and we were packing up, I lifted my rod which I had cast under the willow on the opposite bank, and on the hook was a burbot. I had never before seen this beautiful fish with a barb on his chin, but I recognised it from the school natural history books which I had read and from Brehm's 'Life of Animals'. When I couldn't go to the water for some reason, I was reading at least the pages about fish with as great a passion as my friends were devouring their cowboy books.

So there were burbot here! It was an unexpected surprise. I knew that it was our only fish of the cod family and that it feeds at night, so we prepared for night angling on the very next Saturday. With the following day being Sunday I could sleep later.

Those nights beside the water belong to my most beautiful memories. Near the little dam it was like a great theatrical scene, with the wings built by the moon from the trees and shrubs, and with an orchestra of bush crickets which played on the willows like cicadas. In the murmuring of the falling water from time to time came the sounds of splashing fish, in the distance the hooting of a tawny owl.

Above the dam the surface of the water was like a mirror. shining as cast silver in the middle, while under the banks of bushes the solid darkness penetrated the water, air and alders until everything melted into one. Shining on this velvety deep background were the single spots and whole bunches of leaves glistening like beaten metal.

All at once a dark ring with shining edges which spread further and further flows from under the bushes into the mirror of the water. Just behind it follows another ring of darkness and light, then a third, until the whole surface of the water is in motion. The small waves rebound from the opposite side of the river, floating round the twigs sticking out of the water before returning, weakening and calming until the surface is once more a silver mirror.

Now I hear in the alders a crunch, rustle and gentle splash and in this moment can see in the moonlight the up to now invisible producer of the rings of light and shade - the muskrat. It is like the head of a comet in front of a tail. In itself it does not shine, but around it is a silver line and following behind two rows of glowing waves move further away as the muskrat swims to the opposite bank.

When I feel a jerk of the rod which I am holding in my hand I stop watching the rat and loosen the line a little so that the fish on the end can more easily take the bait, a big earthworm. After a moment I strike, pull the fish towards me and lift it. How many have we already?

Eight. If it continues to go so well we shall soon have our bag full.

I put another worm on the hook and was remembering my first day at school with my unfortunate little rucksack. I had then inherited my briefcase from Stana and he himself had had it in the second class, already well used, from Tatinek. I was still using it for my school books in my second year at the gymnasium, but then our parents bought Stana a new briefcase and I inherited his. After that my old case had been used for all sorts of things. When I was guarding the apple orchard and saw that the perch was too big for my sandwich bag, I repaired the broken stitches in the briefcase and took it for my fishing.

Tatinek catches another burbot, and I feel something jerking on my rod again. It was not a burbot but an ordinary gudgeon. How could it possibly have taken such a big worm? I think of throwing it back in the water, but instead put it onto my pike line with the double hook, hoping to catch some fish on it. I drop it straight into the deep water below me so that it cannot tangle in our rod lines. Tatinek catches another two burbot, but nothing is biting on my rod now.

We look at the time: half past one. The moon has already set. I will try to sleep a little in the haystack which is only a few steps from the dam, but first I must look at the gudgeon on the double hook. I take the line and feel that there is some larger fish on the end. It struggles, but in no time at all I pull it up. It is a beautiful burbot, the largest which we have caught tonight! But now I really must go to sleep. I cannot keep my eyes open any more. Still one little thing though - I fix on the double hook the tail which was left from the gudgeon and drop the line back in the water. Possibly even this will be successful.

At last I am wriggling into the hay. It is a big, tall stack. People make them in the meadows when they have no wooden haybarns. They first of all prepare a circle 3 or 4 metres in diameter, sticking into the ground in the centre a straight pole up to 5 metres tall and laying dry branches about half a metre deep around this pole. On the branches is then piled a tall cone of hay, reinforced by the pole in the centre and isolated from the damp ground by the branches. In between the branches I find a small cavity in which I am completely hidden, head and all. It is true that it pokes and scratches me from all sides, but when one sleeps it doesn't really matter! The only thing that is important is that it is warm. I close the entrance to the cavity with a curtain of hay, and don't know about anything any more ....

It seems to me that I have only just started to sleep when I hear Tatinek:

"Come, the fish are starting to bite again!" He speaks gently so that he would not awake me if I am sleeping too deeply. I feel the care in his voice, as if he wanted to say "I would leave you to sleep still, but I know that you would reproach me." Tatinek has caught two more burbots in the time whilst I slept. I climb out from under the hay, feeling as if all my bones are bruised, but I forget my aches when I am once more by the water.

It is still pitch dark. We should have taken more worms with us. In our bag made out of an old sock there are only about ten left. I am still half sleeping, with the rod in my hands, and I awake fully only when I have a bite. Now it goes much more slowly than it did in the evening. Only small fish, probably gudgeon, are nibbling at the bait. I put another worm on my hook and cast it to the other side. I think it hasn't reached the bottom yet but something is already jerking. Another good burbot, and Tatinek has one too.

I go to him for the last worm and kick a peg knocked into the ground. I had nearly forgotten it. It is the end of the line with the gudgeon tail. If there is a fish on it, it will not run away. I first of all cast with my rod to the opposite side and afterwards pull up the 'pike' line. It is heavy; something is struggling, but differently to the burbot. Burbots weave, this fish is tugging hard. I pull about 1½ metres of the line from the water, but that's all. It is stuck somewhere on the bottom. I jerk the line, I pull, but without success. What shall I do? Certainly not break it.

I take off my clothes though the water is icy cold and my teeth are already chattering. How could it not be cold when the river is shaded by trees and shrubs for almost the whole of its length? The night air does not add much warmth to it. I am already knee deep in the water below the pool, but must go still further. When the water reaches my waist I catch my breath, but am already beside the line. I can see it, for now day is breaking. I take it in my hand and feel around with my foot. I thought so.

There is a root, and the line is twisted round it. Now I touch the fish with my foot. It moves to one side, and the line jerks in my hand. I untangle the line from the root with my foot. What good luck! It is only wound round and not knotted. At last the final turn. With one hand I lift the line, and with the other I am searching for the fish. I feel a big head. It is a chub! - the largest I have ever caught. He must weigh more than a kilo...

In the east the sky is already turning red. We pack up. The briefcase is too small to hold all the fish. Seventeen burbot and one chub! The chub and five of the largest burbot I put onto a string and tie to the handlebar of my bicycle. We go home.

Half of the fish we gave to our neighbours and some of them I sold. With the money which I got I bought a penknife called 'Sarajevo', for which I had been longing from my boyhood. It was a so-called 'dangerous' knife, with a blade as long as the width of my hand, so it could 'reach into the heart'.

My dear Knezdub's dam! How many half days have I sat by you and how many nights nodded there with Tatinek or by myself?! How many fish, experiences and pleasures you gave me! Your virgin crystal waters were as the personification of the dreams which had accompanied me, night after night, for the years when the walks with my fishing rod along the river Dyje were denied to me. Now I no longer dreamed about fish. The reality was more beautiful and stronger than any dream!

By the middle of summer the pool below the dam had

changed into a swimming pool. Children from Straznice and Knezdub were splashing there and from the high wooden wall, on which Tatinek and I had so often sat with our rods, boys were jumping into the deeper water. From time to time the hay cutters were refreshing themselves in the pool too.

It was the end of the quietness and of fishing too. But even without these goings on, my freedom for daily sitting by the water had anyway finished. We had to fulfil the month's working duty which was imposed upon us by the Germans, so my holiday shrank to just the month of July.

One of the many Czechs expelled from Slovakia, just as we had been expelled from the Sudetenland, was the well known potter Mr Landsfeld who came to Straznice and set up his workshop not far from us. When I first had gone there last year to see his work I took a piece of clay, and in no time at all had modelled a cow from it. Mr Landsfeld was surprised that I had never been taught how to do it and asked me to make something else too. So from my hands there grew a lizard and a frog. After that Mr Landsfeld invited me to come at any time and make from the clay anything I liked, but I preferred my freedom by the water and so I didn't take up his invitation at that time.

However, at the end of last November Mr Landsfeld had come to see us. My three little sample figures had proved so successful that he had had many orders for them, and he asked me then to help him produce them for the Christmas market. Mr Landsfeld offered to pay me 3 crowns an hour and I accepted. It was my first real and regular pay.

For the month before Christmas I had worked in the workshop after school, making dozens of figures of cows, lizards and frogs, but this mass production didn't please me very much. Soon Mr Landsfeld's elder daughter joined us, and I was able to do as I preferred, creating new figures - a dog, cat, crayfish, fish, sheep, horse, snail with his shell, and children building a snowman.

I gave all my pay to Maminka. With the growing cost of living each crown was useful and I needed no money for myself - things like sweets, chocolate, roasted chestnuts and other goodies had long since vanished with the arrival of the Germans. My fishing hooks I had already bought, so I completed my tackle only with a whole ball of 'real' string to make pike lines

This year, on 1st August for the second half of the main school holidays, I started work in the pottery again, and now was working eight hours a day. Mr Landsfeld increased my pay to 5 crowns an hour.

At first I again modelled the animals for which there had previously been such a demand, and also added others to give more choice, but soon I devised something different. I made figures from the story about 'The Great Beetroot' which every child at that time knew:

- The old man planted a beetroot, and the beetroot grew and grew and grew. The old man wanted to pull it out, and he pulled and pulled but he could not pull it out.

So the old man called the old woman. The old

woman behind the old man, the old man behind the beet, they pulled and they pulled, but they could not pull it out.

The old woman called the granddaughter. The granddaughter behind the old woman, the old woman behind the old man, the old man behind the beet, they pulled and they pulled, but they could not pull it out.

The granddaughter called her puppy. The puppy behind the granddaughter, the granddaughter behind the old woman, the old woman behind the old man, the old man behind the beet, they pulled and they pulled, but they could not pull it out.

The puppy called the kitten. The kitten behind the puppy, the puppy behind the granddaughter, the granddaughter behind the old woman, the old woman behind the old man, the old man behind the beet, they pulled and they pulled, but they could not pull it out.

The kitten called the little mouse. The little mouse behind the kitten, the kitten behind the puppy, the puppy behind the granddaughter, the granddaughter behind the old woman, the old woman behind the old man, the old man behind the beet, they pulled and they pulled until the beetroot shot out and they all fell on top of one another. -

My group of figures of the characters in the story, the old man pulling with all his might at the leaves, the old woman, granddaughter, puppy, kitten and mouse, was so successful that it was taken as a model for further production.

After 'The Great Beetroot' I made a 'Vodnik' - the 'Water Man' familiar from many Czech children's stories and from Dvorak's opera 'Rusalka' - , sitting on a hollow willow, and then a group of four of the most important musicians in a Slovak folk band - the first and second violinists, the clarinetist, and double bass player.

At this time Mr Znoj was also working in the Landsfeld's workshop. His brother was a professor at a well known school of ceramics in Bechyne in Bohemia, and 'our' Mr Znoj was extremely gifted too, making - on the wheel - plates, bowls, cups, beautifully shaped jugs, and 'Cepaky' - narrow necked vessels for water and wine. Based on my small and simple musicians he modelled similar larger figures, and added a cymbal player too, with detailed working of their faces and country dresses. They were real works of art.

When all the clay work was sufficiently dry it was baked in one of two electric kilns. After the first firing Mr Landsfeld and his wife covered the pieces with white glaze and painted the dishes with the old, traditional 'haban' ornaments of flowers and leaves. The figures were coloured as in real life. After the painting the items were fired again before being carefully packed up and posted to the best shops in the country.

Sadly, later on, Mr Znoj came to an inglorious end. He drank too much and finally committed suicide. What a waste of such a great talent!

In the last week of the school holiday whilst working I was scratching clay from my hands with my penknife. The blade stuck on a drying lump and cut deeply into the flesh below my fingers on my left hand. Mrs Landsfeld bandaged my hand but the blood soaked through, and with only one hand I could not work. So the new knife 'Sarajevo' was really dangerous! But Mr Landsfeld gave me a certificate saying that I had been working for him the whole four weeks so that I could continue my studies.

The work in the pottery workshop had meant the end of my freedom for me, and this I missed very much - especially on nice summer days. I was so much longing to be by my river Velicka! But I was working 8 hours a day, finishing about five o'clock in the afternoon, and so there was even less time for wandering by the water with my fishing rod than when I was in school, when the lessons had finished about half past one. No wonder that I was looking forward to the beginning of our new school year, even though I was not very enthusiastic about the lessons themselves. I was only looking forward to seeing Zorka again; she still had a captivating magic for me. Knowing that I could only expect the ordinary school friendship from her changed nothing in my feelings.

Mr Landsfeld was so pleased with my work that at the beginning of December he asked in school for me to help him again with the fulfilment of his pre-Christmas orders, and the school released me from my studies for a while. During this time Mr Landsfeld suggested to me that I should leave my studies and work permanently with him. He said, too, that his daughters would in time be ready for marriage and that he would like to have me as a partner.

I was not yet fully 17 years of age at this time, and such planning seemed to me much too premature. Certainly I wanted to finish my studies, and anyway I didn't like especially either of the Landsfelds' daughters, nor did I want to give up the freedom of my times by the water which meant so much to me now when all other human freedoms were being abolished or limited to the necessary minimum. When beside the water I could forget in what gloomy conditions we were living, how difficult it was to find even the barest necessities for life, how cruel Fate had been to Tatinek in his work, how even Maminka, who had never been mollycoddled and was used to physical work, had such hardened and cracked skin on her hands from weeks of rubbing corncobs that in the end she could not manage to strip the goose feathers because they stuck so on her damaged fingers. With this work she helped our previous neighbours, the Gajdas, who once again sold us cheap potatoes and corn for flour, so that we wouldn't starve as did so many people in towns who were dependent only on their rations.

All foodstuffs, soap, shoes, clothes, cigarettes, spirits, and even bicycle tyres and tubes were rationed and in very limited quantities, and it was not legally possible to buy any more than the prescribed ration for which we had coupons. Therefore there was a flourishing blackmarket, and cigarettes as well as wine and home distilled slivovice were always precious commodities. So Tatinek kept his ration of cigarettes to exchange for lard and other necessities, and was smoking locally grown pipe tobacco of not very good quality. He had got to know the local farmers who were growing tobacco for the State and they sold him some of it cheaply - and of course illegally. The Germans punished severely the blackmarketeers, but nobody could manage without them.

I cut Tatinek's tobacco and made cigarettes for him throughout the war. The knife had to be razor sharp to cut the tobacco, that was why the Sarajevo had cut my hand so easily. Later he bought a small home made cutting machine, and then the production of cigarettes became easier.

With the new school year another subject was added to our lessons - biology. Professor Sladky, who had been expelled from Slovakia too, taught us. He started his first lecture with the words "The basis of all living matter is the cell - 'celula'". He repeated 'celula' so many times during the lesson that we gave him the name 'Celula' too.

I liked biology most of all the school subjects. At this time all school books printed before the war had already been abolished by the Germans but new ones were not being published, so we had to learn without textbooks. We wrote all the material ourselves, and copied the sketches which the professor drew on the blackboard or made drawings from the printed pictures on posters which he hung up. Because I had grown so much, I was sitting in the last but one bench, and from that distance I could not see well enough what was written or drawn on the board. So I had to go to Brno to have my eyes examined, and then had to wear spectacles - the only one in the whole class!

In a thick writing book without lines I made an

exemplary book of biology, expanding the text and pictures drawn in school with many additional pictures from Brehm's 'Life of Animals', and with a well arranged system showing the development of life from protozoa to the separate genera of vertebrae.

On Saturdays, after our ordinary lessons, another subject was added - dancing. For boys these lessons started in the sixth class, for girls in the fifth. Stana had already been learning for two years, but as a complete 'anti-talent' in dancing his lessons were mostly limited to winding up the gramophone and changing the records.

Because I had no smarter clothes, my parents had a double-breasted suit made for me for my dancing lessons from the beautiful English material which they had bought just before the war. It is true it was not black as most of the other boys wore, but even this blue-grey with a fine stripe gave me lots of selfconfidence, which I badly needed in communicating with girls.

I realised very quickly that dancing was something which was completely natural to me. I danced well and with great pleasure, not missing a single dance and even choosing the older girls as my partners when they were free. Already in the first lesson I liked especially two brunettes from the fifth class - Liba and Miladka. Liba enchanted Stana too, and soon there grew from it a great love between them.

Miladka was small, with a beautiful and perfectly regular face framed in long, dark hair, and I courted her shyly. I wished so much to have a real love. Twice we even arranged a rendezvous in the castle park, but it was something different to the dancing lessons when I could hold Miladka in my arms and did not have to talk. At the rendezvous I was not brave enough to hold her hand, and I was searching for my words without great success.

For Christmas I bought her a book and she gave me a gift too, but I was expecting in vain that she would awaken in me such deep feelings as I still had for Zorka. So after the New Year I wrote to her to explain how it was with me. I thought it would be dishonest to nourish in her, and in myself too, false hopes. Miladka was really unhappy about it. Her friend Liba brought me a message that Miladka could not be living without me.

I was really sorry for her, but she survived this separation, and by Spring she already had another boyfriend from the seventh class, whom she married immediately after finishing her studies.

Since the beautiful July fishing for burbot under the Knezdub dam I had managed to go to the water only for very short periods. Firstly I was working in the pottery and now the whole of Saturday afternoons was occupied with my dancing lessons.

After that, when bathing children drove out every fish from our fishing pool, I searched through the river against the current, and found a few very promising ponds with chub and burbot there, bigger than below the dam, but not so many of them. During the day they lay hidden in the roots of the shrubs lining the banks, and ignored my earthworms. They started to hunt at night, but because there was no haystack there in which I could sleep a while, I never fished there at night. I would cycle there in the late afternoon to lay five of my lines baited with gudgeon. These I caught in my hands from a narrow hole below the dam where they congregated thickly even though the water was disturbed by the children. The fishing was not so pleasant as fishing with my rods but at least I could be, even if for only a brief time, beside my beloved river.

Usually I cast two of my lines into the biggest pond, and in the other smaller ponds the three others. By the time I had managed it and turned to go home, it would be evening already. In the morning I would leave home to collect my lines before school, which started at half past eight. There were always some fish on them - two, three, once even four good chub and sometimes burbot.

It was a wet and cold autumn morning. Because our parents and Stana were sleeping in the bedroom, and I in the kitchen, I could leave bed and dress without disturbing anybody. I did not look at the clock; it was still dark and that was the important thing. I reckoned that by the time I reached the water daylight would be dawning already and I would be back at the usual time to go to school.

But when I arrive at the river it is still pitch dark, with no sign yet of the dawn. I will look at my lines by the light of my electric torch. Possibly there will be something on them already. I wind up the first line; the double hook is empty, even without the gudgeon. It has been torn off by some chub which has not been caught itself. The rain stops. A few stars peek out from behind the clouds.

Winding the second line I see that it leads straight underneath me. At evening I had cast it into the centre of the pool. In the light of the torch I see the water is a little more than one metre deep, full of roots and dead branches on which the line is entangled. On it - good heavens, that is some fish!! A burbot - so big that it looks more like some monster than a burbot! I cannot even guess its weight. How can I reach it? I will go back to the other lines and then see.

The bait on the next line has gone, the second is untouched, and on the third is a chub of about 3/4 kilo which I pull out of the water. The hook is only lightly stuck in his lip, and when I pull it out the chub twists, jumps out of my hands and falls to the ground. I try to stop him with my boot, but the fish slips on the wet grass, jumps over my foot and splashes back into the water. In the beam of my torch I see how he slowly vanishes in the deep water, so I return to the first pool. It is still dark, even though the clouds have vanished, and stars are shining in the sky.

I have lost one fish already. The gigantic burbot I must certainly catch! I shall wait until daylight when I can see him better. Until that time I shall lay down and relax a little. The grass is wet so I lie on the frame of my bicycle which is beside the river. It is not very comfortable, but still better than lying straight on the soaking wet grass.

I realise that I am dozing only when I am awakened by a sudden brightness which touches my closed eyes. Just above me a luminous greenish line is stretching across the sky. I see just the tail of the shining meteor which then rapidly vanishes.

A falling star! They say one should make a wish when one sees it and the wish will be fulfilled. I wish that I will successfully catch the burbot, and I fall asleep once more.

I awake with something tickling my face - it is raining again. The stars are gone and it is already light. How long have I been lying here? I feel cold and sore from the bicycle. What has happened to the burbot? I go to look at him. He is standing on his head about a metre under the surface of the water. I pull the line but it is as if nailed to a strong root near his head by the wire trace which has become entangled with the line. If I want to bring the fish to land it will be necessary to break off the whole root. Now I see that the wire trace has twisted several times and possibly is only holding on the last fine brass wire from which it is made.

I take off my waterproof coat, my jacket and pullover, but am not brave enough to remove my shirt as well; I just roll up my right sleeve and then, lying on the dry lining of my coat, I try to catch the fish in my hand. Even when I have his tail right up near my ear I can reach only about halfway along his body. Because I can't think of a better way I press him, my fingers sinking into the flesh, but they are too short to hold him properly. For the fish it means a new support. He flexes and the last wire of the trace breaks. I try once more to reach him so that my whole sleeve is soaked, but I can touch him only with the very tips of my fingers. I see how he is sinking deeper and deeper in the middle of the pool. Why don't I take the double hook off the other line and try to stick it into his body? Possibly I will be successful. But I have this idea too late...

All at once I am sorry for everything. For the lost fish especially. The chub will recover easily, the wound in his lip is minute, but what about the burbot with the double hook in his mouth? And I am sorry for myself, too, for the mistimed leaving from my bed and for feeling so cold and wet. Not even the falling star helps.

Soon even my fishing on lines ended. I was ill with mumps and lying in bed with a fever.

Already that summer street corners, public buildings, railway waggons and other places were 'decorated' with posters and leaflets saying that "Germany is winning the war for Europe on all fronts." Fanfares over the radio introduced news of the German victories, the surrounding and collapse of resistance of the English forces fighting in France and being pushed back to Dunkirk.

In June Paris fell into German hands, and each day we were expecting the news that the German forces had started to invade England.

In July the Germans started the concentrated bombing of English towns and cities. Daily they announced how many tons of bombs they had dropped there, how many dozens of English aeroplanes had been shot down or demolished on the ground by their invincible fighter-bombers, the Stukas, how many tons of British shipping had been sunk by their U-boats, and so on. We were afraid that the end of European free states was nearing, with the northern parts going to the Russians and the western parts to the Nazis.

From all this misery I was escaping to the murmuring of clean waters which washed away at least for a while the dirt of the German propaganda which attempted to poison us day after day with lie upon lie. By the side of a silent pool I was able to forget the inhumanity of the Nazism which had changed our flourishing country, and other peace loving countries too, into a vast prison with unlimited powers given to the warders and slave drivers to decide our fate and lives, and bringing death and mutilation to the best and bravest.

Near Christmas time we moved from Straznice, and with this was closed another chapter in our family's life. I never went back to the Landsfeld's ceramics workshop and it was necessary to part with the pools of my beloved little river Velicka.

*
* *

Our new home was in Bzenec, a small town 10 kms from Straznice. Tatinek had graduated from the vintners school in Bzenec before the first World War, and now fate blew him back there to the agricultural research station. He was transferred from Straznice in March, once again as an accountant.

In the previous autumn he had already reserved for us a nice newly finished little house in a small street, at the eastern end of Bzenec which was called Olsovec. Running beneath the whole house was a cellar with three rooms; in the largest was a well for water with a hand pump, the second room was for the storage of fuel for our heating, and the third for the storage of vegetables and fruits for use in winter and various other things. In front of the elevated main floor was a verandah from which was the entry to the front hall. A door opened from the hall to our living room-'boys'' bedroom. The door on the other side of the hall closed off a staircase which led to the attic. Beside it were three steps down to the lower anteroom from which led three doors - to the cloakroom, the cellar and the garden. At the end of the hall was the entry to the kitchen and from there were the doors to our parents' bedroom and to the bathroom and laundryroom.

Because the newly constructed walls were not yet completely dry, in the hard frost of -20 C the walls were frozen right through, and inside on the walls and especially on the ceilings there grew thick layers of hoar frost.

From Straznice we were able to bring, besides our furniture, only two sacks of brown coal - lignite - and a bit of kindling wood for starting the fire. Our previous neighbour, Mr Gajda, moved our things, and although his sledge pulled by two horses looked big, it was not possible to load more onto it even when he made the journey twice for us.

The first piece of furniture which we put into our new home in its rightful place was the small stove from Znojmo which had accompanied us everywhere. We started a fire in it, but the cold wet chimney had no updraught. The house filled with thick smoke and we had to open all the windows and doors so that we would not suffocate. The result was the same when we tried to make a fire in the kitchen range. Finally we had to ask for some straw from our new neighbours, and by burning that first at last the chimney warmed and started to produce a proper draught. By ventilating the house the rooms, if it was possible, froze even more!

By evening all our furniture was in place, and Maminka was warming on the kitchen range and in its oven the roof tiles which, when they were hot, she wrapped in towels and put to warm our beds. In our parents bedroom there was no heating at all, but even in our 'boys" room it was so cold that when we went to sleep we stretched more blankets over our duvets.

Although we had heated the whole evening, at night there was frost in all the rooms, the temperature outside being again -20 C, and, on the ceiling, from our breath there grew yet more frost which was falling on us as crystals of ice and was condensing on the covers around our noses as a white, unpleasantly chilling layer. The windows were so covered with ice we could not see through them, and by morning, even under the bedcovers, it was so cold that Maminka left her bed before daylight to light the fire. This time the chimney already had a good draught, and we had no trouble with smoke.

Our supply of coal was vanishing so quickly that we were impatiently waiting for the load of coal which Tatinek had ordered some time before at the mine in Ratiskovice, but the reserves on the tips there were frozen solid so it was not possible to bring it to us. Maminka was saving coal in the kitchen whenever she could to make sure she would have at least some for cooking for a while, but it was essential to have the fire in the small stove in our room so that we had somewhere where we could be warm.

After two days, when we had put into the little stove the last shovelful of our own coal, we borrowed two bucketfuls from our neighbours.

The next morning, Christmas Day, a big sledge stopped in front of our house. It was full of lignite, and our worries were over! The coal was in big 15 - 20 kgs pieces. The coalman took them from his sledge and put them through the low window in our cellar where Stana and I were taking it to Tatinek, who in turn set it in a neat pile along one side of the room. The coal had to be broken into small pieces with an axe before it could be used for heating, and from that day on that was my task.

Of our Christmas gifts that year I remember only the jerseys, which our Aunt Milka had knitted for Stana and for me, and the load of coal. They both warmed us for a long time afterwards.

Our garden was joined at one corner to the garden of the Anselmi's, who had a small house in the parallel street next to ours. Mr Anselmi, a descendant of one of the Italian labourers who had built the Czech railways, was working in Bata's shoe factory in Zlin. His wife not only looked after their household, but also their smallholding, rabbits, poultry, and the pig. They had a son, Pepa, who was about 12 years old.

Soon after we had moved in to our new house we said a few words over the garden fence to the Anselmi's, and after Christmas they invited us to a pig-killing supper. They had killed a largish pig, and even though they had had to give to the State a prescribed proportion of the lard, meat, and skin from its back - called 'krupon' and used for making leather - there was still plenty for their own consumption and for our entertaining, too. It was really magnificent.

After a very strong soup we had baked 'sparrows' - pieces of meat - with cabbage and dumplings, and we drank real lager from the pub. I had not eaten anything so good for a long time. The 'sparrows' were flavoured with golden fried onions and garlic, the cabbage was glistening with fat, the dumplings were as light as feathers, and I even liked the lager.

In fact it was the first time that I had really drunk an alcoholic drink. The wartime beer was very weak, without much alcohol, but even so I felt the two glasses of it and the adults, who drank considerably more, must have felt it too because there was lots of talking and even singing that evening.

When we parted later on, we carried with us a hamper with a small can of the strong soup, 'obarka', a few liver sausages and black puddings.

Only when we got home I felt sick, and in no time all the tasty delicacies were gone from me. Such a waste! I had not tasted such a rich and delicious 'pre-war' meal for ages, but I did not have the pleasure of it for very long. I went to bed with a slice of dry bread and a cup of herbal tea...

The Anselmi's became our very good friends, and they continued to give us a pig-killing hamper every winter until the end of the war. Maminka used to help them from time to time with tasks such as rubbing off the maize for their animals and at pig-killing time cutting and rendering the fat into lard. Even the other residents in our street with whom we had no close contacts remembered us on the occasion of their pig-killings with some liver sausage or black pudding. There was a really friendly and sociable atmosphere there.

Mrs Anselmi also showed Maminka how to brew 'beer'. The basis of it was well roasted barley malt, which was also used at this time as a substitute for coffee. A watery decoction of malt, after cooling, was mixed in a demijohn with a bit of sugar and yeast, and when the fermentation had nearly finished it was bottled and stored in the cellar. Two or three days later the brew was nicely sparkling though it was practically without alcohol and tasted as very weak malt coffee. It would not keep for any length of time, going bad after only ten days or so, but Maminka used to make it each week, so we had a permanent supply in our cellar.

The winter school holiday was prolonged indefinitely after Christmas. Masses of snow fell, the frosts reached - 3O C, and on the road from Bzenec to Moravsky Pisek there was such a blockage that the road was impassable. A workparty was organised to try to dig through the drift; each family had to contribute one man with a shovel.

The drift was about 150 metres long and 4 metres high, and after a whole day's work only a narrow corridor was opened in it, and that only for a short time. Fresh snow fell was swept into it by the strong wind, and finally the opening was buried under an overhang of snow which collapsed from the top. We returned to our homes at nightfall. Next morning there was no trace at all of our work - the corridor was once more filled to the level of the surrounding snow. We were unable to clear the road that day either. The wind and snow strengthened, so we abandoned the task for several days until the blizzard had blown itself out. After we did finally manage to dig a way through, the piles of snow from the drift still lay by the sides of the road for a long time even after the arrival of Spring.

1941

Coal holiday - Our household - Drawing competition - Marie - Stavnica - Lost ring - Corn harvest - The burbot - Big ditch - Stana in Brno - Glass engraving - Class representative - Zdena - Class party - Tatinek in Mutenice - Night guard

After New Year Mr Gajda came on his big sledge to visit us and to see how we were getting on in our new house. He brought with him 'our' two sacks of flour hidden on the sledge under straw and hay. Only now had he managed to smuggle the corn in and the flour out of the mill. He told us that on the road, some way beyond Straznice, he had passed two German customs officers who had waved and called on him to stop, but Mr Gajda had pretended that he could not understand, laughing as if he were stupid and waving his hand too, but he let the horses gallop on with the sledge. We were so glad to have the flour, but also sorry that he could not manage to bring us potatoes too, though in the hard frost they would most likely have frozen on the way. He promised that he would sell us some in the Spring.

In order to save heating the Christmas school holidays were prolonged, and later the classrooms were only half heated so that we all sat at our benches fully dressed. I had my track suit trousers under my winter trousers.

At first we went to school by train, but it meant

leaving our beds before 6 o'clock because the railway station was a long way away and the train went on a roundabout route through Veseli where we had to change trains. The journey took so long and was so bitterly cold without heating in the carriages that travelling was real purgatory. Later, when the worst of the winter storms had finished, we travelled straight to school by bus, or when the snow on the road was hard and sprinkled with sand I went on my bicycle. My parents had made from an old overcoat and rabbit skins a pair of mittens for me which were long enough to cover my wrists really well and bought me a pair of secondhand tall boots (they cost 500 crowns!) so my hands and feet kept beautifully warm. With the pedalling I kept so warm that over my suit I wore only a thin rubberised raincoat which protected me against the wind.

If heavy snow fell over night I went to school on my skis, inspired to do so by my classmate Milan who lived at the opposite end of the town and was an excellent ski runner. In order to ski the 10 kms to school I had to leave my bed about an hour earlier than when I was bicycling, leaving home when it was still dark, and then my rucksack of books seemed to feel heavier and heavier.

However, skiing was much slower and more tiring than cycling, especially going home after school in the afternoon when the snow was melting and stuck to the skis so that we could only trudge slowly along. It was difficult too when the surface of the track was already icy and slippery, without fresh snow, or when the ice had been sprinkled with sand. More than once we had to take our skis on our shoulders and walk home. Milan was a kind boy, and when he was with me he always took my rucksack of schoolbooks to make it easier for me.

A further disadvantage of skiing was that I was only lightly dressed for the journey so I would not sweat too much. In the classroom afterwards I got really chilled, and caught such bad flu, with chronic inflammation of the remains of my tonsils, that I had to stay in bed quite a long time. I missed so many days of school that, even when I tried to catch up with the lessons, I was not able to bridge the gaps in those subjects which were dependent on a methodical system, such as higher mathematics, trigonometry, French and Latin grammar. I was physically so weakened that I was excused from doing athletics and physical excercises.

Stana was less energetic and travelled by bus until the Spring, when the road was already clean and it was easy to use the bicycle.

However, even this unpleasant winter passed. Tatinek ordered a load of good manure so that we could dig and fertilise our garden which had been uncultivated until this time, plant potatoes and garlic, sow lettuces, carrots, parsley, peas, onions, and all the other necessary vegetables. We also had room for two beds of flowers. Tatinek planted raspberries beside our neighbour's fence, and then made lots of cuttings of white chrysanthemums with which we filled one complete bed. On the other flower bed were dahlias, carnations, gladioli and a few roses - Maminka always liked to have a vase of cut flowers on the table.

We also enlarged our menage with cages of rabbits. Tatinek built them at the end of the yard between the house and the garden. Mr Anselmi had several rabbits, and he lent us a pregnant doe, which we put into the first cage. After the birth and weaning of her six young, we gave the doe back to Mr Anselmi.

We also added six goslings and five pullets to our livestock on the yard, so later we were partly self supporting, having our own rabbit meat, eggs, and the specially valuable goose fat.

The coming of the animals meant more work, looking for fodder for them. Maminka was fed the goslings with finely chopped young nettles mixed at first with hard boiled eggs, later with potatoes. I used to pick the nettles from the banks of the river Morava, which I had to cross by a bridge on my way back from school; veritable forests of them grew there, especially near her 'blind arms'. No wonder that the goslings grew rapidly, though as they grew they needed incredible quantities of the nettles.

Because we were adding potatoes to the goslings' feed, our reserves of them dwindled rapidly. We were hoping that in the summer we would already have our own supplies from the garden, but we did not have enough to keep us until that time. It was not practical to ask Mr Gajda to bring us a sack of potatoes and thereby lose a whole day's work so I offered to collect them from him and bring them home on my bicycle. It seemed a good idea because in the Spring every farmer is overwhelmed with work.

The Gajda's still had plenty of potatoes, so they sold us a sack with pleasure. They helped to lift it onto the cycle so that the sack was partly lying on the bar and partly on the handles, and I started slowly on my way home.

Through Straznice I wheeled the bicycle, walking on one side of it. I started to sit on it only when I had got beyond the town, though I could pedal only with my knees stretched widely apart, and steering with the handles weighed down by the sack was extremely difficult. How clever I had been to pump more air into the tyres before setting out! The cycle was, with the half hundredweight plus, overloaded. At the slope above the river I had to get off the cycle and push it. I thought I would not be able to manage, but using all my strength I just did. There was only one more rise after that from the railway to Hodonin, not so steep as the first but so long that halfway once again I had to get off the cycle and push. The rest of the way was level. Near Bzenec it even sloped gently downwards. At this time I realised that the front wheel was beginning to wobble from side to side, so off I had to get once again. The weight of the sack on the handlebars was too much. The nuts holding the wheel in the fork and bearings had moved. I tightened the outer nut as much as I could with my hand so that I would not lose it, at the same time balancing the cycle and the load with my other hand. To tighten it properly I needed to use two wrenches, but for that I would have to have both hands free. The question was, how could I move the sack from the bicycle and then lift it back on again? I could not do it by myself, and so I had to lead the bike even on the downward slope, tightening the nut again from time to time. When at last I arrived home I was so exhausted that I really had to use the last of my strength to push the cycle the 15 metres from the main road to our house and lean it with its load against the wall. Completely shaking, I had first to regain my breath and only then could I move the sack, with Maminka's help, from the bicycle. She took most of the potatoes to the cellar in a bucket, and then she lifted the rest in the sack onto my back so I could take it to the cellar too. With this my potato 'anabasis' finished.

Maminka ensured a source of food for our rabbits by picking young thistles and dandelions from the nearby fields, but, when Tatinek brought home a buck, rabbit numbers increased so much that this food was insufficient and we rented from the town a piece of ground alongside the stream, called Syrovinka, where Maminka cut the necessary grass with a sickle. In summer Tatinek scythed the grass there, Maminka dried it and either Stana or I carried the resulting hay home on a wheelbarrow, where it was stored in the attic for the winter.

Even the keeping of poultry and rabbits was controlled by the Germans. As soon as the officials were seen in one part of the town the news of their arrival spread from house to house like wildfire. People were hurriedly catching any chickens which they had in excess of their allowed number and putting them in sacks which they had previously prepared for such an emergency, rabbits followed in wooden boxes, and these 'illegal' animals were hidden in attics, barns, cellars and even in woodpiles behind the yards. Each family was allowed to have only two breeding female rabbits, five chickens and six geese or ducks, all other animals being confiscated. As we were 'self supporting' we had no ration cards for meat or eggs, but by intensive feeding and having one extra 'illegal' doe we managed to produce enough meat for our needs. The geese we kept especially for their fat. Maminka fed them on maize in the Autumn so they were well covered. After killing we had to give a certain proportion of the fat to the State and surrender our coupons for rationed fats, but even so it was better for us that way because instead of margarine, which was disgusting, we had our own excellent home produced fat.

Once again, as in her childhood, Maminka was gathering dry pieces of wood from the forest. There were large pine forests nearby which were good sources of supply of dry branches and pinecones which she collected in bundles and sacks and brought home on a wheelbarrow. She took with her a long pole with a hook to break off any higher dry branches from the trees. Taking a saw to the forest was illegal.

Maminka was not alone in collecting wood from the forest. Many families helped their heating supplies in this way, so the forests were neat and tidy with floors covered only by a thick carpet of pine needles. Without lying branches or cones and with the trunks of all the trees cleared of dead wood, the forest looked more like a carefully tended park.

The forest also supplied us with resin from its pine trees; Tatinek and I collected it because it was already not possible to buy pure resin for making soap, and that made with the pine resin had a pleasant aroma of turpentine. The smell of bought soap was so foul that Maminka didn't even want to wash our socks with it. She preferred to make her own from carefully collected rabbit fat, resin and lye as Mrs Anselmi had shown her.

In the Spring the town bank ran a drawing competition for the youngsters, the entries to be anonymous. I think the age limit was 18. I participated in it, entering a drawing in soft pencil the very ancient lime tree in the castle yard, and a second scene from the castle park. The judges gave the first prize to my lime tree, and the second to my park scene. When it was discovered that the first two prizes had been won by the same person I was invited to the bank. The Director congratulated me, saying that both the drawings were by far the best but that it would not be very tactful to the other participants to give two prizes to the same person. He asked me for my agreement that my second prize should be annulled, the third prize winner should be placed second, and the fourth placed third.

What could I do other than accept this solution? I was given a savings book with a deposit in it of 50 crowns and the bank kept the drawing of the lime tree, so in fact it bought the drawing for 50 crowns. All the same I was happy about it. The picture was framed and hung in the banking hall.

In the cinema in Veseli they were giving Walt Disney's film 'Snow White and the Seven Dwarfs', the very first whole evening's colour film to be shown on our screens. It was such a sensation that I went on my bicycle to see it too. I left the cycle with my schoolmate, Dana, who had two younger sisters. One of them was ill with jaundice. When, after the film - which was really something completely extraordinary - I came to Dana to collect my cycle, I asked for a glass of water to quench my thirst.

In a few days I also had a fever and jaundice. I must once more stay in my bed and stick to a strict diet. It seemed that one illness after another was pursuing me so that I could not keep up with my school work.

At the end of the school year there took place the first social event in which I could take part. It was the 'prolonged dancing lesson'. It differed from the ordinary lessons in that it took place in the evening. The girls were in beautiful long dresses, and their mothers were present too, sitting along the longer side of the hall and critically observing their own offspring and, even more critically, the other youngsters.

Miladka already had another boy as her partner, and Zorka was never free, so I was circulating with the girls without much choice - dancing only for the pleasure of the rhythmic movement. It was possible to improvise whilst doing the foxtrot and the tango, and this gave me a special satisfaction, finding that even in dance it was possible to create something new. I was looking for the 'lady's choice'. Who would come for me?

Once it was Stana's classmate, Marie. She was two years older than I, very plain and ordinary, but she pressed herself so closely to me that I could scarcely breathe. We made a perfect pair in which neither one of us was leading; we were only absorbed with the rhythm of the dance. She was the best partner with whom I had ever danced - it was as if in a dream. I felt her small, firm breasts on my chest, and was only sorry that I had not discovered her sooner. We did not say a word to each other, but after the 'lady's choice' I asked for her twice again and she chose me once more. Clearly she was pleased by my company too. That was the last time I saw her.

Many years later I learned that she had never married and remained a spinster.

Half way along the road on which I went to school a large bridge crossed the river Morava, built here instead of the former ferry, though the place was still called 'the ferry'. Not far beyond, on the Straznice side, was a smaller bridge under which passed the backwater in which were the pools called Vesky and Prachar. This water I could see ran through dense forests, parallel to the Morava. Once when I was looking for nettles for the geese I, unable to resist, went along a path on top of the protecting river wall, into the unknown, hoping that there I would find some nice place for fishing.

The dark water, shaded by the crowns of the trees and bushes, didn't attract me at all, but suddenly I came into full sunlight at the end of the forest, and to the left, below the wall, appeared the glittering waters of the river Velicka. The canalised water ran straight into a large lagoon where the river swung sharply to the left. One could still see the old bed of the river going straight into the Morava, but, I wondered, who could guess what might happen when the wild spring waters looked for a new route?

On the left bank of the Velicka rose the wall of forest, on the right was a meadow with willow bushes and a jungle of nettles two metres high. From the lagoon the water meandered between wild banks, sandy shallows with fast flowing waters interspersed with dark pools from which jutted out stumps of sunken trees until, at the end, below a cliff more than ten metres high, the river was absorbed by the wide and strongly rushing Morava. This untamed, unconfined part of Velicka was called Stavnica.

The first large lagoon looked so promising that one beautiful sunny Saturday Tatinek and I went there to try it.

We settled on the steep bank above the lagoon, whose waters flowed slowly some two metres below us. Tatinek had an ash rod onto which I had fixed a long line so that his hook and worm could fall to the bottom of the pool near the beginning of the lagoon. I with my bamboo rod and reel angled lower down. Good perch were biting, the largest being about ½ kg. We already had five of them when I had a really strong 'take' and I hooked a larger fish which ran from the end of the pool into the stream. What luck that I have the reel on my rod and can loosen the line to the fish! I start to tremble from the tension. Such a fish I will not be able to throw out of the water as I had thrown the perch, and so I climb down below the pool, skirting round a bush which is shielding my view, into the shallower water and easier access to the river. I can still feel the fish on my raised rod. At last I am beside the water, playing the fish and bringing it nearer so I can see it in the shallower water. It is not, as I had thought, a chub, but slimmer, beautifully golden and it is pulling down towards the bottom. Now I manage to lift its head from the water, it turns from side to side, but I bring it to me. A good barbel! Not so big as I had expected from the strength of its fighting, but it is my first barbel!! The hook is holding only in the corner of the tough mouth, but I only take it out when I am sitting behind Tatinek a safe distance from the water. Compared to the barbel which I used to see before the war in the river Dyje it is only a beginner, but even so it is a beautiful fish. It looks a bit like a large gudgeon with not two but four barbs beside its mouth, and it will certainly weigh more than 1 kg.

After that we caught some more perch, and in the late afternoon pike were hunting, splashing lower down the river. When Tatinek caught a gudgeon I cut the hook from my line and fixed on a wire trace instead, with the double hook from my pike line which I always carried with my tackle in case the occasion should arise when I could use it. I baited the hook with the gudgeon and went down to the end of the backwater where I laid it in the shallow water and weighted it down with a few handfuls of sand. I then walked back to our lagoon, at the same time releasing line from my reel. When I came to the spot where I had landed the barbel I rewound the line onto the reel so that it just stretched across the bend of the water. I pulled with the rod, felt that the gudgeon was released from the sand and with the tip of the rod near the water I slowly reeled in the line. I realised that I should have fixed some small weight in front of the bait so that I could lead it more deeply through the water, so I stopped reeling in and waited until the bait had dropped to the bottom, which showed by the dipping of the line. Then I started to reel in again, stopping after about 10 metres so that the gudgeon dropped deeper once more, continuing these 'jumps' right across the backwater. When the bait reached the middle of the water and as I started to reel in, the line stretched, I struck, and out of the water jumped a good pike. In those first few seconds I could hardly believe that I had hooked the fish, but he jumped again shaking his head. I saw the gudgeon fly away from his open mouth, but the hook held.

And so, for the second time that afternoon, my hands were shaking as I played the fish. It fought differently to the barbel, which had held to the bottom of the water with concentrated resistance. The pike darted with unexpected rushes so that I had to give him extra line from the reel from time to time, and then bring him nearer. But finally he stopped fighting, and when I lifted his head from the water he lay inert, enabling me to land him easily with my bare hands.

When he lay in the grass beside Tatinek he seemed to be not so big as the pike from Prachar's pool, about 1½ kgs in weight. But it was my first pike caught on a fishing rod, and playing him was much more thrilling than catching pike with pike lines.

As I had no other small fish which I could use as bait for pike, I cut off the wire trace with the double hook from my line, and fished once more with worms on an ordinary hook. Soon came the time when we should pack up. When Tatinek was pulling his line out, his ash rod bent like a bow. In the middle of the boiling and splashing water there showed a tremendous pike's head, with nearly a span's width of body. At that moment the rod shot up, the pike had cut the line and was gone. Such a fish! Such a pike!! It must have been at least 5 kgs in weight - no wonder that even Tatinek is shaking!. And it took only half of an ordinary garden worm...

Now there was nothing else to do, only to pack and go home. Even so, we had a beautiful catch of four kinds of fish - about fifteen good perch, a few rudd, my first barbel, and my first pike caught on a rod.

After the experience with the monster pike I thought that Tatinek should be angling with better tackle than he had and so, now that I had my own money from working in the ceramics workshop, I went on my bicycle to Veseli where I bought a good 2.5m long 'tonkin' bamboo rod in two sections with leading eyes, and the simplest aluminium reel. When I gave it to Tatinek he was so moved that he was utterly speechless. In the shop I had also bought a whole 100m spool of 'imitation' line and a spinner, which had a lead head, red beads on the shaft, and finished with a red wool tassel on a treble hook. The main spinner was on the shaft, one side was polished copper, the other silver. I wanted to try if I would be successful by pulling it through the water like the gudgeon. The ash rod we now kept only for fishing for small bait fish.

The next Sunday morning Tatinek and I cycled to Stavnica to fish again in the lagoon, but the fish were lazy. I was hoping that we would catch some small fish which I could use as bait for the big pike, but the water was as if bewitched. After some smallish perch nothing moved at all. Tatinek went to try in a pit left from the old river bed on the other side of the path, and no more than half an hour passed when he caught a nice, almost ½kg tench. I put it in our keep net and dropped it into the water. In fifteen minutes Tatinek was back with another tench of the same size, so he initiated his new rod with two golden fish.

I was sitting patiently by the pool, but the floats on my two rods did not move at all. In the hope that the pike would again take a worm, I fixed the hook on the bamboo rod with a steel wire trace, but the pike ignored the worm just as the small fish ignored it. Finally I stopped fishing with the worms; instead of the hook I put my new spinner on the trace and, as I had done with the gudgeon, I went to the end of the backwater, weighted down the spinner with sand, came back to the pond and reeled in the line with my 'jumping' technique. Soon I felt a tug. I struck, but I landed only a half rotten willow twig. The spinner with the lead head was heavy and dropped to the bottom. I left the spinner to lie where I was standing, went back around the bend and was spinning with the flow of the stream, but again some rubbish stuck on the hook. After that I tried how the spinner was working in the water and I saw that for good spinning I must reel in more quickly and without the jumps. So I went back to the lagoon and reeled once more against the stream. In the middle of the bend I felt at last a take, I struck and this time it really was a pike! I easily brought it to land, it was only a small one, not 1kg in weight.

There was no path there and I had already had enough of trudging round the water, tripping over dead branches and bushes growing by the water's edge, falling into holes in the ground and struggling through the jungle of nettles in which were hiding clouds of mosquitoes. It was not easy at all. I tried combing the lagoon with the spinner, but the new 'imitation' line which I had pulled from my reel onto the ground in front of me got into such a mess when my cast lifted it that I could not manage to untangle the line and had to cut off the damaged piece, rejoining it with a small knot. This made spinning so difficult that I gave up trying it and went back to fishing with worms.

In the afternoon we added only a few small perch and one rudd to our keep net, so we packed up and cycled home.

After that I went to Stavnica twice by myself, and each time the gamekeeper caught me there. When he asked me if I had a licence I showed him my permit from the fishing club, but he said that this water belonged to the castle and the permit was not valid there. The first time I easily got away with this mistake, but the second time he was already not so friendly. Even so I still went there once more.

My classmate Mirck, with whom I talked about Stavnica, told me that good catfish were biting there now. He said he would talk to Mr Novak who had a fishing permit from the castle, and that he would take us there with him one Saturday night. I should bring with me plenty of lobworms and we would meet at 7 o'clock at the bridge.

I got to the place already well before 7, but Mirek didn't arrive. Even after another hour he hadn't come, so I bicycled to Stavnica by myself. I would certainly not return home when I was prepared for night fishing with such beautiful lobworms!

This time I didn't stop at our lagoon, but went on to the high cliff where the river Velicka ran into the big river Morava. There was already another fisherman there for night fishing. I left my bicycle and tackle not far from him and went back with two strong lines, crossing the Velicka at the shallows. At the mouth of the little river I cast my lines with a good part of the worms. Only when I returned to my 'camp' did I make ready my bamboo rod and start to fish.

Holding the line with the fingers of my right hand, I felt that some small fish were nibbling one worm after another, but I didn't have one really good bite. Darkness was falling quickly; possibly it would be better in the night.

Time passed slowly, but nothing happened. I asked my neighbour what time it was. Half past midnight. Even though I was well muffled in my old coat I began to feel colder and colder; possibly it was partly the result of not sleeping. From time to time my senses switched off, but I was still sitting and holding my rod, and even heard loud splashes as if somebody was hitting the water with an oar. So the catfish were hunting, but completely ignoring our hooks. It is true that once or twice my rod jerked, but I struck no fish. The line was too long and I would be no more successful even when wide awake.

In short, neither of us caught anything, and in the morning the mosquitoes started to bite again. To cap my misery we were surprised by the gamekeeper, who didn't like it one bit when he saw me by the water again. I tried to argue that I was not fishing in Velicka, but in Morava, and therefore I did not need a permit from the castle, but he said that this part of Morava belonged to the count too, and the other fisherman agreed. With that I felt completely entrapped. The keeper wanted to take my rod away, and said I could talk when I came to the castle for it. Now, at last, the other fisherman intervened, saying I didn't know that I was fishing in prohibited waters and he should not make such a terrible todo of it. So he calmed down a little and said I should pack my things at once and go home.

I didn't need any further encouragement. I had had more than enough of this unsuccessful fishing. I reeled in my line, collapsed my rod, fixed it to my bicycle and left. When I came to the ford I pulled my trousers up above my knees, took my cycle on my shoulders and waded to the other side. I went back to the lines I had laid the previous evening. I re-wound the first - it was empty with a clean hook, but from the cliff came the cry of the official "So you are even laying lines here too!" and something about the unfortunate result of catching me. I was laughing, because in his heavy boots he could not cross the water, but I didn't know about his dinghy.

Whilst I was still winding in my line he stopped swearing at me and started to run upriver. As I was winding in the second line he was already in his dinghy, pushing it with a pole to my side of the water. What luck that I had seen him! It would be easy for him to cut off my way out! I threw the lines into my bag, jumped on my cycle and hurried back along the path. Certainly he was nearby already, and so when I came to the ford I carried the cycle once again across the water. I could see him amongst the bushes bordering the path and hear his unpleasant and threatening shouts, but was already climbing up the steep river side, jumping on the cycle and, standing on the pedals, cycling hurriedly away.

So I parted with that beautiful and promising spot in a hurry. I never went back there again; I was not longing for another encounter with the gamekeeper.

Zolina had her kennel in the corner behind the verandah, protected from the wind. One May night I was awakened by her whining. When it had continued for some time I went to look outside. Zolina had a boy friend there, a little brown dog of about the same size as she. It was a mystery to me how such a small dog could have jumped over the metre high wire fence which enclosed the garden, but clearly even dogs' love has no barriers. Next morning Zolina was alone again, her lover having left as he had come.

In July Zolina had five puppies. She looked after them most carefully, licking, cleaning and nursing them, and the puppies grew into fat, squeaking bundles - later into gambolling, frolicking and wrestling little dogs.

When the time came to part with them, Stana's girlfriend, Liba, took one, a dog puppy, to whom they gave the name Zolik. Three of the others found new homes in Bzenec, and the last was reserved by our 'uncle', a small holder whose name was Blecha, with whom I should work during the harvest to fulfil my work duty.

This family link happened thus:-

In Polesovice our Aunt Marie died after a long illness, and Uncle Albin was left alone with two small children, a boy Tonek and a girl Anezka, who still needed a mother. Uncle's largish farm felt the need of a housewife, too, and so Uncle had no other choice but to marry again. Our new aunt was from the village of Skalka, and the match-maker was her brother, Blecha. An unusual story preceded this change in Uncle's life.

At the beginning of the Thirties Uncle Albin and Aunt Marie were drying hay on the meadows in Ostroh and, whilst raking the hay, Aunt lost her wedding ring. There was no sense in looking for it - the meadow was large and any hope of finding it minute, as looking for that proverbial needle in the haystack.

The hay was dried, raked, stacked, and brought home by Uncle on the horse drawn waggon to Polesovice, where it was stored in the barn.

Fifteen years passed, and Aunt died. That Spring when Uncle was ploughing one of his fields, he noticed something flash in the new furrow. He picked it up. It was the lost wedding ring. It had been carried with the hay from the meadow to Polesovice, then from the barn to the stable, from the stable to the dunghill, and finally to the field where it had lain, being turned with the soil for fifteen years. During that time, the ploughshare marked it with a deep scratch, and in the end it was lifted into 'God's light', as we say.

People said that it was a good omen, and so my Uncle married again.

When we were talking about the fact that during the

main school holiday I should fulfil my work duty somewhere, word got around, and the matchmaker Blecha showed an interest in me.

So. when corn harvesting began, I started as an agricultural worker in Skalka with Blecha who had a small farm. The Latin proverb 'Nomen - Omen' ('In the name is the portrait of the character') fitted him very well.

Blecha means flea. He was small, nervous, and a real parasite. Too talkative, he was a hypocritical bigot whose energy was concentrated in his tongue and who left nobody in peace. He was not very enthusiastic about work; for that he had his strong, well built wife who slaved like a horse and did not say two words the whole day. A smile never showed on his wife's round, reddish face, which was always shaded by a scarf below which hung a braid of ginger hair. Her scared eyes were always cast down. If I sometimes caught her glance, there was in it some emptiness and a complete resignation. They had no children, she carried this misfortune as an unforgivable fault, and Blecha treated her like a barren cow. Dressed in a skirt, with the scarf on her head, and in a simple flaxen sleeveless blouse which exposed her round arms and under which swelled her full breasts, was as if she had walked out of one of Manes' drawings (Manes was our greatest romantic painter of peasant life). She cut the corn with a scythe. I took it away, bound it in sheaves, and carried the sheaves to Blecha who stooked them. When we took the corn from the field, Blecha's wife lifted the sheaves onto the waggon where Blecha stowed them, and I raked any corn which was left under the stooks. Blecha told me many times that as a student, I had no idea about agricultural work and therefore he wanted to teach me about its difficulty so that I could fully appreciate the reward which he was going to give me for it.

Lunch was a snack eaten in the field or in the barn in which we were storing the corn, and consisted of a slice of bread with lard and raw onion or pickled cucumber. We drank sour milk. Blecha drank beer.

There were two kinds of supper. A piece of chicken or smoked pork, which Blecha ate out of our sight somewhere; for us there were potatoes in white sauce flavoured with vinegar, of which I could take as much as I liked, he said, or cucumber sauce with potatoes, cabbage with potatoes or dumplings with plum sauce. Blecha did not take much on his plate, always saying that he was not hungry. On the first Sunday, when Tatinek came to see how I was progressing with my practice, there was smoked pork with cabbage and dumplings, and Tatinek was invited to eat with us and even given a glass of beer!

By the second week my trousers were in tatters; the knees, rubbing against the sheaves, were worn through. Blecha lent me a pair of old trousers made from a rough hempen cloth which survived even a third week. I had no energy or wish for more than that, and anyway the harvest was finished. I returned home even thinner than before, but in new trousers which Tatinek bought for me so that I did not need to come back looking like a tramp.

Later Blecha brought us a 20 kgs sack of flour and

told us how, with great difficulty, he had saved the flour for us and how dangerous it was for him to bring it to us. Of course, my parents paid him for it. He promised that later he would bring us 'something more'. To my great displeasure he took the last of Zolina's puppies; after that Zolina would not eat for some days and, especially at night, she howled.

In the autumn Blecha brought us a sack of potatoes, and once more we paid him for it. We asked him how was the puppy, and we learned that, chained to its kennel, it had barked so much that Blecha stabbed the poor little thing with a hay fork and killed it. It was the last time that we saw him. We rejected any of his 'help' for the future, but Blecha was still for a long time boasting how he was, during the war, 'supporting' us and had thus saved us from hunger.

Later Tatinek's schoolmate from the vintners' school, Mr Jurecka who lived in Bzenec, was really helping us - substantially and unselfishly. He sold us potatoes and second grade corn and maize for the chickens and geese for a very reasonable price, and also such excellent milk that from the cream which she managed to save Maminka sometimes even charmed a little lump of real butter, making it in a jug! Later he was selling us even the corn for our flour, managing to smuggle it into and out of the local mill with his own corn, so we did not need to buy it from Straznice any more.

At the beginning of April General Rommel started a

new German offensive in North Africa. At the same time the Germans also attacked Greece and Jugoslavia, and then in June the Soviet Union. We bought a large map of Europe and were marking on it how one Soviet city after another was falling into German hands. As the Eastern front progressed so died in us the last remaining sparks of hope for some miraculous salvation.

After the corn harvest I spent all my spare time fishing. Already in the Spring, when I was cutting the nettles for our goslings, I had discovered new and pleasant waters in our neighbourhood. They were a little further than Velicka or Bata's canal had been from Straznice, but on my bicycle I reached them quite easily, and most important of all they were far away from that gamekeeper.

I had noticed one place on my way to the film 'Snow White', and I had looked at it still better when I went to buy the new rod for Tatinek. It was the overflow canal which crossed under the road to Veseli and which took the flood waters from the upper part of the Morava, bringing some of them from the town of Ostroh to save it from flooding, to join the river again under the Vnorovy dam. At the time of the Spring and Autumn floods masses of muddy water ran straight along the bed of the canal carrying whole trees and branches, planks, bodies of dead animals and many other things which had been in their way and not able to resist.

In the summer clean, warm water flowed slowly there, moving the fine, wavey sand on the bottom as the wind moves dunes in the desert. The water hardly reached to my knees, and in some places not even to my ankles, so that no one would believe that two months previously it had been a furiously rushing element which had endangered people's lives and property.

I discovered there were burbot in this clean, gentle water. They were hiding under the tree trunks brought there from somewhere upstream by the floods, under rocks and the concrete ashlars which had originally reinforced the sides of the canal but which, unable to resist the attacking waters, had been torn from their positions and washed into the middle of the bed.

I was catching the burbot just with my hands. I was soon able to recognise under which boulder a fish would be because, at the entrance to the place where the fish was hiding, the sand looked as if it had been swept, with no trace of the mud which usually settled on such places, being clean, sharp and jagged, and it was sufficient just to put my hand in the crevice for my fingers to touch the smooth body of a burbot.

No one who has not caught a fish in his hands can understand the thrill of the moment when the fingers are sliding gently on the fish, when they touch the head, when they are turning the fish so that it is possible to hold it behind the gills and bring it from under the rock into the light. Possibly it is not sport fishing, but surely in every man is a touch of the ancient hunter or herdsman. Those who have the herdsman blood in their veins cannot understand the feeling of the huntsman when he is hunting and has a catch. To this category belong not only the huntsmen and fishermen, but collectors too who keep their catches in albums or display them in glass fronted cabinets, who are seeking fossils, stamps, cacti or antiques - each 'catch' they feel as a thrilling adventure. Perhaps that is why collecting, as is hunting itself, is usually a characteristic of men rather than of women.

I did not fish for the main result of fishing - the fish, even though the extra food was especially welcome in this miserable wartime, but I was always excited by the direct contact with the mysterious world of fishes, imagining the life under the water, playing fish on my rod, or feeling the question of the moment when my hand was dipping under a rock or tree trunk - would a fish be there or not? How big would it be? Would I be able to catch it? And when my hand held a good fish which my fingers could hardly encompass, the catching and pulling it out was so thrilling that I was not even aware of how I was scratching the skin off my knuckles on the sharp edges of the fish's hiding place.

When the burbot I touched was small I left it in peace, so probably it did not even realise that it had been in some danger. Sometimes it happened that the fish which I had already squeezed then managed to escape through another hole under the rock, but I could easily reach it in the clear water so it was not wasted. This fresh water member of the cod family is a night hunter and in the daylight was obviously so dazzled that it would swim only a few zigzagging movements away, and then stop and press itself to the bottom. When I approached it slowly so that my shadow did not fall on it, the fish would stay in the same position and I was able to grab it.

One Saturday afternoon, enticed by my first successful catch of burbot, Tatinek came with me too. We left our bicycles on the river bank, together with our trousers, shirts and sandals and clad only in our underpants we went into the warm water. I showed Tatinek where the burbot would be hiding and how I caught them, and then we walked slowly upriver against the flow, Tatinek on one side of the water and I on the other. When Tatinek found a burbot he usually called for me to catch it. Sometimes, when there were several escape routes under a boulder, we fished together, one on each side. After some hours our keep sack was full, so it was time to go home.

We climbed out of the water and went back to our bicycles. When Tatinek was putting on his shirt he said that he thought his back had been burned by the sun. When I looked at it I saw that he was very red right down to his waist, and that his shoulders were one huge blister. I had not been wearing a shirt throughout the whole summer, but this was the first occasion on which Tatinek had been so exposed to the sun. At this time Tatinek wore braces to keep his trousers up, so he pulled his braces over his burned shoulders and we cycled home.

The journey must have been sheer torture for Tatinek, but he never made one word of complaint. As soon as we arrived home he pulled off his shirt - and with it the skin peeled from his shoulders, having stuck onto his shirt. The braces had scraped bleeding stripes, blisters had developed on the whole of his back, and he had sunstroke and a temperature. Maminka put Nivea cream on Tatinek's back, and through the night he had to sleep - or, more accurately, be lying - on his stomach, naked, while Maminka cooled his back with cold compresses.

Next day, Sunday, the wounds on Tatinek's shoulders had dried a little, and on Monday he went as usual to his office. Later the skin on his whole back peeled off, and the scabs which formed on his shoulders where the braces had rubbed were still cracking and bleeding for some considerable time. Tatinek was braver about his own pains than anybody I have ever known.

Of course that was not the end of our joint expeditions for the burbot, but Tatinek was more careful afterwards and kept on his shirt. The fish we caught were not very big, 600 grams was about the largest, usually they were about 300 - 400 grams, but they had superb meat, few bones and large, very fine livers which were a real delicacy.

Further downstream a bridge for the Bzenec to Veseli railway line stretched over the canal. One of the stone piers supporting the steel construction of the main bridge rose from the centre of the canal. The stream of water striking the pier had gouged a hole in front of it over a metre in depth, and this was covered by a mat of branches, grasses and twigs which had collected in front of the pier in the previous floods. One could almost always find some good burbot, perch or chub in the brushwood, and so I went there in the near certainty of finding a fish.

Half a day spent floundering around, even in only knee deep water which felt warm, was still cooling my whole body, and I did not much like to go into the deeper water. I would go when it was necessary sometimes but on tiptoe, so that I would wet as little as possible of my body. When the water current washed away the quicksand under my feet, my position did not feel very stable.

It was just so on one special day. The weather was not very warm, and when I bent so that I could reach with my hands under the wreath of brushwood, I gasped because, whether I wanted to or not, I must soak my chest too. When my hand touched a round, scaly body I held my breath. Probably a chub. It is more sensitive than the burbot . Now, when I only just make contact it moves a little forward. I already know where is its tail. With the other hand I try to find the head. It is between a thick branch and an ashlar of the pier. I am touching the fish as gently as I can. It is big and must weigh at least 2 kilos. It does not stay quietly - when I touch its tail it moves a few inches forwards, when I touch its head a few inches back again. I cannot reach it with both my hands, having in front of me the pile of brushwood which gets in the way, and I can reach its head only with my left hand in which I have neither the skill nor the strength that I have in my right.

I judge where would be the gills of the fish, and I

squeeze hard. But the fish is quicker than I, and I feel how it is escaping between my fingers. It shoots forward, knocks into my left knee so hard that I lose my balance and, waving my free arm, I splash into the water and not one hair on my head remains dry.

That was enough for me! I did not look for the chub any more. Who knows where it might be already, and in free water I could not catch it anyway. Such a fish! The biggest chub which I had ever had within reach of my hand and I was not able to catch it!

The number of good sized burbot in the canal was diminishing, and therefore one day I went on my bicycle downstream to explore its right bank, until I reached its junction with the river Morava below the dam which held the water for Bata's canal.

The Morava was a large river flowing into the Danube, and the fish there were correspondingly big too. I knew that the depths there were catfish weighing even as much as 100 kilos, in the fast running waters stood barbel as big as logs, and below the headlands were noisily beating asps weighing five kilos or more. What a pity that with my rods of mountain ash and bamboo these fish were inaccessible to me!

I tried to fish in a smaller and quieter backwater, but even there the current was so strong that it was carrying my baited hook into the rocky shallows at the river's edge, so I caught only a few small roach and Danubian yellow ruffe.

I set out for home before sunset, and to shorten the

distance went on a path across the meadows, hoping that I would come to the road on which I travelled to school.

After some time, noticing a nice group of trees which stood in the middle of the grasslands and thinking there could be some water under them, I turned towards them, pedalling with more energy to get there in the shortest possible time. I was right. I found a part of the forgotten arm of the Morava, the 'Big Ditch', lined with willow and alder bushes from which arose larger trees, with only a couple of clear places which gave entry to the water. There was a big pool at the end of the arm with a good spot in which to sit. I could not resist and, even though it was growing darker, unpacked my rods to try my luck there.

Already with my first cast I caught a good perch, then a second, third, fourth, fifth, sixth! And between them were two larger roach. This was the water for which I had been longing! Possibly it could become my kingdom, such as I had in Vesky. There were so many pike there too, the centre of the pool seething with the hunting fish, and splashes echoed again where the pool narrowed to continue as a meander amongst the meadows.

At last I had to stop fishing because I really could not see the float any more. I did not know the way home, and could only just see the path, a slightly lighter line between the grasses, but happily it brought me to the road. I arrived home only when it was completely dark.

Next afternoon found me once more sitting by my newly discovered water. As in Vesky, where I was catching the tench two years before, here too was a little plateau just above the water, and at my back a cliff two metres high hid me from the meadows, so that I was in complete peace there.

As bait I am using small, red worms. We have plenty of them at home under the heap of compost from the rabbit hutches, and in such hot summer weather it is difficult to catch the bigger earthworms. That morning I had managed to dig up only one of them from our garden. Today mostly perch are biting, but they are smaller than yesterday's and not so many. Perhaps I have already caught the bigger and the flock of them is thinner. I am casting to the same place, to the right of the brushwood which I think must be under the water, though only a few dead twigs show on the surface, and in which I am sure the flock of perch is taking cover.

At last another bite! The fish is taking the worm carefully. Possibly it will not be a perch this time because a perch would take the whole worm at once. Only now does the float run across the water and slowly sink. Still a little further - the line is already stretching. I strike, and a small perch flies onto the bank. I was mistaken. Luckily the hook is stuck only in its lip. I return it to the water, and put another red worm onto the hook. It looks as if now I am just feeding the fish, the tiny fry nibbling off the soft bodied worms and I have in my keep net only six perch and three roach. I must pack up and go home. Yesterday I got home very late, and my parents were worrying about where I could be for such ages.

I put my five last red worms onto the hook . The float shows that something is again nibbling at the bait, but in a short time even this stops, and when I take out the line the hook is empty, stripped clean. So I put on it half of the only earthworm which I had brought with me. First the tail half. It makes a splash when I cast it, being so big. In no time at all the float moves, jumps and sinks under the water. It could be something large! But again I land only a small perch. How could it possibly take such a large bait? The worm is so damaged that I must put the second half on the hook. I cast a little further from the sunken brushwood, perhaps there will be no perch there. And indeed, ten minutes pass and the float is standing completely still, without movement. The sun has set already and I am looking at the reddening sky but, when my eyes turn back to the water again, I see only how the float is vanishing.

I am already holding the rod and striking, but the rod stops halfway, as if the line is stuck down there on some root though I see that the stretched line is still moving. It is cutting through the water so that it is hums on the rod, and making straight for the underwater branches. No - there you cannot go! Now the line snags on some drowned twig. If I lose the fish I will never again to the end of my life take a rod in my hands! Please, God, let me land the fish! See, I can even pray in such a difficult moment! Now I manage to turn the fish from the dangerous brushwood, but it runs in the opposite direction towards the reedbed. I could lose the fish there too! Just in front of the reeds it turns and goes to the deep water in the middle of the pool. How lucky that I have a reel on this rod - I must loosen some line, otherwise it will snap. No other fish has fought so hard on my rod. What could it be? A carp?

At last it stops and I pull it slowly nearer to me. It is still struggling, zig-zagging from side to side, but I bring it to the bank. It is a tench - but the size!

The fish still tries to get free in the shallow water, but I catch it behind the head with my hand and bring it up on the grassy bank, a safe distance from the water. Now that I can see it clearly it does not look quite so big - not in comparison to its strength in fighting - and is different to the golden tench from Vesky, being a dark, purplish black. How heavy can it be? It is much bigger than the heaviest tench I have caught up to this time, the one for which I was swimming on that morning in Vesky. I will weigh it when I get home and will see.

I pedalled my cycle with great pleasure through the meadows. My bag was once again full.

The tench weighed 1.8 kgs, so it was my biggest fish caught on a rod up to that time, and it is still, even today, my record tench.

On Skarpa was such peace and quiet and, for the whole time I was fishing there, so few people passed along the path by the water I could count them on the fingers of one hand. They were the farmers looking at the grass on the meadow which, every year flooded and fertilised by the waters from the river Morava, gave the best hay in the country.

One day at haymaking time, when it was so hot that even the fish were not biting, the floats scarcely moving, I caught only three roach which I kept for Tatinek's pickling.

Around me rustles a dragonfly. Tiny fry are nibbling in the weeds in the warm water near the land. I am watching the fragile bodies, how jerkily they are moving. All at once a robber darts in between them - a cigar-long young pike with large eyes. With its vehement attack ruffling the water, I cannot see if it catches his prey. The fry scatter and hide in the weeds, only those at a safe distance ignore the little pike. But it is enough that the attacker comes near them, and the fry swim away in a fanshaped pattern, clearing the field.

My observations are interrupted by an unexpected voice:-

"Are you fishing?"

"Yes, I am". I look at the path behind me, and I see a girl, about fifteen years old, wearing a bright red skirt and white blouse. In this solitude she seems to me to be really beautiful.

"May I come and look?" she asks.

"Come!" I invite her to climb quietly down to me. "I will show you something - a baby pike!"

When the girl was sitting beside me I am stealthily observing her sweet, charming face, fine and perfect complexion, long eyelashes and beautifully curved lips. But I am mostly looking in front of me, showing the pike which, flushed, swims a little further away. The girl is looking where my finger is pointing, but she cannot see the tiny pike. She lowers her head towards mine, so that I feel her hair on my cheek. She notices the fish at last and sits up again. What a pity! She asks me about everything, and I feel unusually happy in her company.

One of the floats moves, and our conversation stops. I strike and land a small perch. The girl rejoices -
"A fish!"

She wants to play with it, but I take it from her hands.

"Be careful, it will prick you!"

She is surprised that a fish might prick. I show her the hard, sharp spines on its dorsal fin, and she carefully touches it with her index finger, at the same time asking hundreds of what seem to me to be silly questions. I take the hook out of the fish's mouth and release it in the water.

After half an hour the girl says she has to take her leave.

"I must go. My parents are carting the hay, and the waggon will be loaded already..."

I watch how she, in her wooden clogs with their burnt in pattern of flowers, is climbing up the bank. On the path at the top she stops, looks at me with a smile, and in the next moment is gone.

I sit for a while, as if unable to waken from a dream. She appeared and vanished again, just like a fairy. Was she not an illusion? I climb up the river bank too, and far away I see a flower - a red and white little figure. It wasn't a dream. What a pity she has gone! It would be so nice to be sitting by the water, just the two of us. It was so beautiful when I was taking the perch from her hands and our fingers touched!

A few minutes later I look at the meadow again. The red and white flower has gone. Maybe after all it was just an unattainable mirage...

At the weekends Tatinek usually came with me, but we didn't catch any larger fish on our rods. If we caught a small roach I used it on a pike line which I cast on the opposite side where there were no shrubs. I remember when I caught the first pike. Tatinek noticed that the big cork on the line was dancing wildly, and by the time that I had run round to the other side of the pool I was so breathless through excitement and running that my heart nearly jumped out of my body.

I caught five or six of the pikes there; they were not big, only up to 1½ kilos. The real giants were hunting by the side of the bushes where I could not reach them.

One day two fishermen came from Brno on a motorcycle with a sidecar. They carried two long bamboo poles with forked ends, a pile of strong lines and two buckets with bait fish. They were able to reach easily over the bushes which were for me an unsurmountable barrier. They put the bait fish on double hooks, set a line in the forked pole and laid it exactly where they wanted it to be just as if they had laid it there with a long rod. After that they slipped the line from the fork, so that it lay neatly over the bushes, fixing the end to the nearest branch. Thus they laid about 20 lines. They walked from one line to the next, with their poles easily releasing the lines from the shrubs and landing the caught pikes, then resetting their hooks with bait fish. And so it continued through the whole afternoon.

I don't know how many pike they caught that time. The sidecar of the motorcycle was filling up, and because I could no longer bear to watch it, I packed and went home.

Next Sunday the fishermen came to the water again, and the whole process was repeated, with the only difference that the catch was not so rich that time.

By the autumn the water was empty, without pike. Even today I remember it with bitterness, but with a twinge of jealousy too. How many of the dozens and dozens of pike might I have caught myself?

At the time when I was toiling at the harvest and enjoying my fishing, Stana was working in the office of a local builder, so he was already earning his own salary. After the main holiday he went to Brno to study on a two years' course at the school of building industry, and then there arose a new difficulty.

He was lodging and eating, with two other students, at the home of a widow, a leech for whom her lodgers were a productive well of income - not only in terms of money, but in material goods too. Because of the shortage of lodgings at this time, Stana was glad to have a roof over his head, and therefore we had to buy for the widow, on the black market, food ration coupons, sugar, cigarettes and lard, for which she was especially hungry. Luckily the father of one of my classmates, Mirek, was a butcher, so he was able to help us from time to time. One kilo of lard cost 500 crowns - and that only because it was out of friendship, otherwise we would have had to pay still more for it. Even so it was astronomically expensive, but we were glad that we were able to buy it.

This was still not enough for the monster-widow. Stana had with him in Brno his own bedding and feather eiderdown. The widow changed Stana's new sheets for old, and even stole from the eiderdown so many feathers that she left not half in it. Maminka discovered this only when Stana finished his studies and brought home the eiderdown. She could not recognise it, it was so empty.

When Stana first came home he brought me a box of coloured pencils, called 'Technicolor', and that gift started in fact my real painting creativity.

On his next visit he brought a set of six stemmed wineglasses. Our pretty glasses, decorated with festoons of cut leaves, had disappeared somewhere during our moves from Znojmo, and we had only simple 'tasting' tumblers for our wine.

I liked the new glasses for their pleasant shape, but remembering our old glasses it seemed to me that they were asking for some decoration. I wanted to engrave something on them for Stana so that I would lose the feeling of indebtedness and would repay him for the coloured pencils. I already knew that the carborundum sharpener for our sickle would scratch glass - Tatinek had successfully smoothed with it the chipped end of a wine sampling tube - but with the sharpener it was only possible to do rough work on the glass, not fine engraving.

So I broke a piece off it - leaving most of it for sharpening the sickle - and chipped that piece into smaller bits, from which with a pair of tongs I shaped chips which were pointed at one end. These I fixed with thread onto wooden holders which I made from pieces of split pine wood, and so my scribers were ready. I experimented with them on a piece of window glass, and then started to work on the wine glasses.

It was a really wearisome job. The points of the carborundum chips wore down so quickly with the pressure on the glass that even after only three or four scratch marks I had to use another scriber or, if it was still possible, reshape the used chip with the tongs to make a better point so that I could engrave another millimetre of my design. This labour taught me patience, which is so necessary in fishing too, because my design was very rich. On each of the set of six was on one side a complicated monogram S M framed in a shield, and on the opposite side was a figure depicting one of the tasks in the vineyard or the cellar. Both elements were joined by garlands of vine leaves and grapes.

It was work without end. For each grape I must scratch about thirty times, and therefore change the scriber many, many times, so in order to manufacture them I had to use nearly the whole sharpener. But I finished the set successfully, and gave it to Stana for

Christmas. I think even today that this, my first big glass engraving work, is of quite a high standard.

At the beginning of the school term came the election for the new class representative. Last year Fanus had held the post, this time my schoolmates elected me so clearly I had already grown into the collective, even being a member of the elite group, the 'Strong Seven' which was the moving force for all the activities of our class. To be the class representative was actually chiefly only an honour, because links between the students and professors were minimal.

For Natural History we had a new course of lectures - Somatology, science of the human body. Professor Sladky - 'Celula'-, was our professor again, and his teaching technique was so perfect that he awoke a real interest in this subject amongst all his pupils. The lectures started with the anatomy of the skeleton, followed by the muscles, internal organs, circulation of the blood, nervous system and glands. The part about the sex glands 'Celula' read to the girls and separately to the boys.

Because we had no text books for this subject, I made a similar book for Somatology as the one I had made for Zoology. The basis of it consisted of my drawings of bones, muscles and all the other organs and details with their Latin names. Later I was very glad that I knew the subject so well.

Dancing lessons started again. Miladka already had her boyfriend, Palos, as her dancing partner, so I was never so brave as to ask her to dance with me. The older girls had left the school, and with them my excellent partner Marie, and now we were joined by some younger girls amongst whom was Zdena, the two years younger sister of my classmate Dana.

Zdena was a slim, extremely beautiful and attractive girl with brown-blond hair falling to her shoulders. Dana was pretty, too, but Zdena possessed that gift which created around her in the dancing lessons a flock of boys to whom she gave generously of her smiles. She was very well aware of her magic, and it was no wonder that I liked her too.

She was completely different to the wise, equable, almost motherly Zorka or the quiet and introspective Miladka. Her blue eyes were sparkling with vitality and the provocation of her sixteen years of age, her laugh was rippling like a stream in Spring.

Once Dana arranged a rendezvous for me with Zdena on the meadows in Veseli, and Dana came with us. The second time Zdena didn't come. In the dancing lessons she shone for me like a shooting star, but she went with other boys.

Much later I learned that Zdena married very young, even before she had finished her studies. One day her husband surprised her with a lover, and stabbed her to death with a kitchen knife. Such a tragedy, a terrible waste of a beautiful girl, and total desperation of him who loved her so much!

Our class still continued with our practise of singing

in the breaks between lessons. The repertoire consisted mostly of Slovak folk songs, but sometimes we would sing some contemporary songs too, like 'Pity of Love' by Jaromir Vejvoda, which later became known throughout the world as 'Roll out the Barrel' and happened to be adopted as their own by the English and American armed forces.

The enthusiasm for singing was so strong in us and the pauses between the lessons so short that we decided to organise a class singing party. After the grape harvest, a room was booked by Fera at his uncle's place, and everybody who could brought a bottle of wine or something to eat. As the spokesman for the class, I asked our class master, Professor Zurek and our teacher of Czech language, Professor Huska, to participate in our party. Thus we were under official supervision and so the gathering could not be taken for some anti-German conspiracy.

Of course the 'Strong Seven' were there - the three girls, Zorka, Zdena and Jirina, and the four boys, Fanus, Fera, Milan and myself, as well as most of the class. From amongst the other boys we invited the violinist, Slavek, who came with his first band of second violinist, clarinetist and cimbalist.

Our class master left early, but Professor Huska stayed with us to the end of the party, and so it happened that he became the 'patron' of our future parties.

The whole evening was filled with singing, accompanied by the music, drinking wine - the first time I had tasted it - and the occasional solo boy's dance, the

'Verbunk', in which both Milan and Fera excelled, as did of course Slavek, who later became the great authority in the field of Slovak folksong and music.

The male dance 'Verbunk' expresses youthful power and elation and has no strict rules, being pure improvisation. The lad sings one verse of song of a given rhythm, then dances this same melody accompanied by the music, jumping, twirling, gesticulating with his arms, clapping his hands either together or on his high leather boots, then singing the next verse and dancing again, and so on.

There are literally thousands and thousands of old folk songs in Slovenia and Moravian Slovakia, each one more beautiful than the last - real jewels of national creativity both musically and poetically.

I was the unwearying dancer of the 'Odzemek', a dance performed with bent knees. I danced to the end of the longest song, and after that just as long as the music played, though the other boys had tired already and fallen out.

We parted after 10 o'clock and I, still full of joy, was cycling home. I even opened my rubber-lined raincoat, I was so hot. When I came through the little gate to our garden, Zolina barked once, but I calmed her and slipped into the house as quietly as a little mouse so that I would not waken anybody. Next day I had a slight headache, but my legs hurt much more - they felt the 'Odzemek'!

Tatinek did not stay for long in his new office. On

1st September 1941 he was transferred to the Wine Research Station at Mutenice where the Director was Ing. Vobr, who had moved there after the German occupation of the Sudetenland, straight from Znojmo.

Mutenice was a village about 40 kms from Bzenec, so Tatinek was able to come home, by train, only for weekends. He found lodgings in Mutenice with the Srameks. He had lived with them twenty years before, when he started in Mutenice on his expert wine research career.

The Srameks were rare people; they looked after Tatinek better than if he had been a member of their own family. Mr Sramek was a brick layer, who worked with such speed that he needed at least three assistants to mix the mortar and supply him with bricks, so he was extremely busy and everybody who needed such work to be done asked him to do it. He charged very little for his work, but appreciated being given plenty of cigarettes and wine. He worked as three men, and drank and smoked as three too, smoking 100 cigarettes a day and drinking three litres of wine without showing any symptoms of drunkenness. He ate little; perhaps the wine gave him so much energy.

Mr Sramek was tall and lean, his wife short and round. Having when young been the cook at the vicarage, she cooked excellently even in these years of shortages, and she was very pleased that Tatinek appreciated her dishes so much. At the end of the week she used to pack some goodies for Tatinek to bring to us - cakes, Christmas sweetmeats, or delicacies from the pig killing. Tatinek showed his gratitude with gifts of tobacco, cigarettes and wine.

The German offensive on the Russian front had continued with giant steps since the summer. When they started to attack Moscow we were tensely expecting to hear the news that she had fallen, which it seemed to us would be the prelude to the collapse of all Russia. Luckily hard frosts militated against the insufficiently equipped Nazi forces, and their attack on Moscow was halted by 4th December and then stagnated for the whole of the winter.

On 6th Decmber the Japanese attacked the American base of Pearl Harbour in the Pacific. America then proclaimed war on Japan, Germany and their allies, which kindled in us a new ray of hope. America would help Britain and possibly some turning point in the war would be reached which would lead to the liberation of Europe from Nazi slavery too.

The Germans decreed that all villages and towns must provide night watchmen from amongst their local citizens to guard against the activities of saboteurs and terrorists. Our night watch consisted of about a dozen members. Every family was obliged to supply, according to a rota, one man who had to come twice a year on a fixed day and at a set time to a meeting place from which were allocated to each pair of men the streets which they should guard.

Tatinek did his first turn of duty in the summer; in

winter he was in Mutenice and Stana was in Brno, so that the only male member of our household able to undertake this duty was I. Because neglecting this duty would be punished, when my turn came I dressed warmly, taking Tatinek's old but still warm fur coat and in my breast pocket a small, flat bottle of plum brandy - slivovitz -. In my right pocket, for my own self defence, I put my Sarajevo knife which I had carefully sharpened. Thus equipped and armoured I went to the meeting place.

The town was as if without life, sunk in darkness, only here and there was a chink of light showing through the blacked out windows. It was freezing so hard that the snow crunched drily under my boots and the Milky Way sparkled in the sky. Some men were already at the meeting place. We went to the railway station where, in the small waiting room, the iron stove was glowing red hot. One of the guards, marking off our names on his list, asked me why my father had not come. I explained that I was the only man left in our household. The other men discussed something amongst themselves for a while and then told me to go home. Knowing that the public notice proclaimed that 'Neglect of guard duty will be strictly punished' I said that I could not go home. At last they told me that I should wait in the waiting room, keep the fire burning in the stove and that one of them would come for me later.

They left, and I was alone. I waited, but nobody came for me. I put the last shovelful of the coal into the stove and lay on the bench. By midnight the stove was hardly warm any more, and cold was sneaking into the waiting room. I went to the front of the building, but there was not a living soul anywhere, only the sound of a barking dog somewhere in the distance. As I breathed my nostrils were freezing together with the sharp frost, so I returned to the waiting room, had a sip of my slivovitz and crouched once again on the bench. The cold penetrated deeper and deeper into my body.

Only about 4 in the morning did the door open, and two members of the guard came in. They were very cheerful, and with their arrival the room filled with the strong scent of wine. They were very surprised that I was still there, and firmly sent me home with the words that they would guard for me! They went with me to the main square and there they turned away down the street of wine cellars.

I went on home, bruised, sleepy and chilled to my bones. Later I learned that a substantial number of those vigilant night guards found asylum in the cellar belonging to some watchful member of the 'anti-diversant homeguard'.

For Christmas we again had a small tree which stood in the verandah, shining with chains of minute white of egg meringues baked onto long threads. Our traditional Christmas tree decorations had been lost somewhere during our moves from Znojmo, but this tree dressed only in Maminka's meringue chains looked really pretty too. There were not many gifts under it; the greatest gift was that we were all together in good health and warmth.

Another great gift, which only then reached us via the 'underground' radio broadcasts of the B.B.C., was the news that on 12th December the Soviets had started a counterattack on the eastern front. The German forces were paralysed by frosts of - 50C, unable to move their motorised units or tanks in such conditions, and the Soviets, on the southern flank of the front which was at that time 1,000 miles long, recaptured Rostov. In the centre of the front they broke through the lines surrounding Moscow. It was the first defeat of Hitler's panzer units; we wished so much for more such news.

1942

Winter studies - Oil paints - Assassination of Heydrich - Gigantic pike I - Forest worker - High treason letter - Class party

The winter of 1942 was perhaps even harder than the last, but we were well prepared for it at home. The fuel part of the cellar was full of lignite and Zolina was sleeping on a blanket in the corridor, her kennel beside the verandah being buried under a deep drift of snow.

In frosts of - 30C many of the trains could not move because the cold cracked their steam tubing, the main coal deposits were frozen solid, and passenger trains were restricted in number so that the coal which was already in store and therefore possible to handle would be sufficient to move the locomotives being used for war transports. So at Christmas there started a 'coal holiday' more than two months long.

Masses of snow fell. In the town everybody cleared it away from in front of his own house, snow ploughs were pulled through the streets by two pairs of horses, and the snow from paths and roads was piled in huge heaps by the roadsides. From time to time I had to go with other 'brigade workers' to clear the snow. We loaded it with our shovels onto big sledges which horses pulled to the frozen stream Syrovinka, on the banks of which in summer we had been drying the hay for our rabbits.

We went to school only once a week so that we

could hand in our homework, and for the teachers to give us new exercises to do at home. There were no school books for the lessons, and it was only possible to write in pencil in our classes because the ink froze in our fountain pens. The conditions for learning were really very bad.

For my 18th birthday, 23rd February, Stana brought me from Brno a magnificent gift - a big wooden case with 35 tubes of oil paints, a palette, brushes, two spatulas and a small bottle of turpentine. It was the most beautiful gift I had ever received and I could not stop looking at the two rows of tubes with their coloured labels and some names which, until then, were unknown to me. It reminded me so much of my fascination with the pieces of pastels given to me 14 years before for Christmas by the artist Budik. Once again there were the pure colours, but now I had the whole new and untouched set, and the case smelt of linseed oil and turpentine. The paints were produced by a young Czech firm, Tapal, and were of excellent quality.

In addition to the paints Stana bought me a light easel, a book about painting techniques by M. Hegr, and a metre of canvas made, because of wartime scarcity, from thin strings of paper with an unpleasantly smelling primer which was already peeling. Because I felt that the preparation of this 'canvas' was not safe for painting on, I never used it.

From Hegr's book I learnt some theoretical knowledge, but I didn't know anything about practical painting with oil paints. In fact, except for Budik's pictures which we had at home, I had never seen any other pictures close to. My only schooling in this discipline were postcards, and prints of pictures by the painter Kalvoda which I liked. These were for sale in the paper shops at this time, and I bought some whenever I saw them. I never tried to copy them, I just looked at them and tried to understand the artist's way of looking at the landscape, to discover something from the pattern, colour and light composition of the picture, and to see the picture as a selfcontained creative unit.

My very first work in oils I painted on 11th March 1942. It was a small picture on paper, of a track between fields, and Stana gave it to his girlfriend Liba.

Painting on paper which was too absorbent was difficult and so I was buying offcuts of plywood from the small local furniture factory, being the only material which I managed to find as a base for my pictures, and even these proved very difficult. It was impossible to buy the glue which was needed to prepare the primer. When I explained this to the owner of the factory he gave me two tablets of dark and smelly wartime glue - he himself had nothing better. He could not sell me a larger quantity of the plywood, which was in very short supply for the factory, but he recommended that I should try in Uhersky Ostroh where there was a large factory making veneers and plywood.

There I managed to buy about twenty pieces of plywood and even some of the powdered glue, though before I was allowed to do so I had to explain for a long time why I wanted the materials. The plywood and glue were important war materials and I, not being a member of any artists' organisation, had no right to buy these things.

I made a sort of harness out of saddle girths for my box of paints so that I could carry it on my back whilst cycling, and added to it a clever system of wire hooks and strings so that I could also carry my wet picture on it. I fixed the easel to the bar of my cycle, a collapsable fishing stool on the back carrier, and bicycled around the countryside, painting and selling my pictures.

It was also necessary for me to fulfil my school duties, and so the only time I had left for fishing was on the occasional Sunday, when I went with Tatinek who was already 'caught' with the love of fishing too.

On 27th May we heard from the radio the shocking news that in Prague the Commander in Chief of the S.S., Reichs Protector R. Heydrich had been assassinated. A reward of 10 million crowns was offered for the apprehension of the assassins, who had been sent from London by aeroplane and dropped by parachute into the Protectorate. Heydrich's successor, K.H. Frank, declared martial law throughout the Protectorate, saying that anyone who helped in any way or hid the assassins would be shot, together with his whole family.

The German occupiers were affected by some kind of madness, daily shooting to death any Czech who 'approved of the assassination'. One careless word was sufficient to warrant the death penalty, and they organised raids to search for offenders in houses, whole streets and villages.

Whilst doing a house to house search the S.S. found in the village of Lidice near Prague an old shotgun and some other old weapons which were not licenced. They had nothing to do with the assassination, but the village was charged that her inhabitants had helped the killers. On 9th June all the men of the 483 inhabitants from the age of 16 upwards were shot, the women were taken to concentration camps and there liquidated, and 81 children were transported to Poland where they were all, near the little town of Chelmo, gassed and buried in a communal grave. The whole village of Lidice was razed to the ground and levelled, and its name removed from the map.

Through the treason of one of the parachutists, lured by the 10 million crowns reward which was offered, seven of the assassins were traced to the church of St Charles Borromeo in Prague. After a battle lasting several hours, when their ammunition was exhausted, they all finished their lives themselves rather than fall into the hands of the Germans.

On 24th June, in the settlement of Lezaky, an illegal transmitter was found. Lezaky, too, was levelled with the ground and the 34 inhabitants, 14 men, 14 women and 6 children were shot.

More killings followed. 15,000 Czechs were shot to death, and even more were arrested and sent to concentration camps.

1942

The Germans behaved in the Protectorate according to Heydrich's words "This space (Bohemia and Moravia) must become German territory and the Czechs, after all, should not be here anyway." Included in the German plans for reorganising Europe after the war for the next thousand years was the elimination of the 'races of less value', the Slavs - that is to say Poles, Czechs and many of the Russians - were to be transported to Siberia, where they would serve as slaves. At last then would be fulfilled the ancient German wish for 'Drank nach Osten' - 'expansion to the East'.

Meanwhile the Germans were sending Czech men to Germany to slave in their factories and to build the Atlantic wall...

How was it possible that even in this time of unimaginable terrors the sun was still shining, the birds and the bees still flying from flower to flower, and the countryside was still so beautiful?

Beyond the canal in which we had last year been catching the burbots in our hands, we discovered a new body of water. It was quite a long way from home, but it was perfectly quiet and undisturbed there. Not a living soul would pass us all day, and in this haven of peace it was hardly possible to believe that at that very moment, elsewhere, people were being slaughtered.

It was, once again, one of the blind arms of the river Morava, similar to the 'Big Ditch', and possibly it was a continuation of the same old river bed. I called it 'The Wattle' because part of the river bank had been strengthened with poles and branches. Most of the water was in the shadow of the forest; the sun shone only onto the middle of the big pool, and usually there was standing, only just below the surface of the water, a group of large chub, much bigger than those which had been in Velicka.

I never managed to catch any of them though. When I cast my line near them they vanished into the depths. After several unsuccessful attempts I moved further along, where the water was bathed in sunshine, between the meadows. Here too there was a good pool where I caught perch and rudd and sometimes even smaller bream and chub. I used to sit on a highish bank above the widest part of the pool, while Tatinek fished where it began.

One afternoon I caught about five good perch, and after that nothing happened for a long time. I cast my line to the other side of the pool, but the float stood still even there. When nearly half an hour had passed, I started to wind the line very slowly back onto the reel, hoping that some fish might be lured by the moving worm. The float moved gently across the water towards me; when it came near the middle of the pool, it changed direction, at a right angle. Just as slowly as I had been pulling it towards me, now it moved to the left. What could it be? A perch? But I saw no jerk on the float, and it moved another metre further on. I struck the rod, but the hook was stuck somewhere in the depths. Probably some small fish had pulled the hook under a drowned branch. I pulled the line and felt the weight at the end move. I pulled harder. It was difficult, but even so I lifted something heavy inch by inch.

All at once my eyes start from my head. Is it a log of wood or a fish? I see in the water a shadow much more than a metre long. Now I can see clearly the head which has reached the surface of the water. A pike - the queen pike! looking more like some dream monster than a fish, with an enormous head and yellow eyes. I realise that the hook is fixed on a thin monofilament line, at that moment the water heaves mightily, the rod lashes upwards, and the black shadow is gone. She has bitten through the line.

My knees are shaking. I cannot even wind the rest of the line onto my reel because my fingers are trembling so. I must sit down. Such a fish! Such a pike, and she took a worm. I feel I have lost a fortune.

A long time passed before I calmed down again. Only then did I go and tell Tatinek what had happened. He said that he had heard the splash, but he thought I had thrown something in the water.

The next Sunday we were by the water again. I brought with me three strong pike lines with wire traces. I baited them with small rudd, and caught a small pike weighing not quite one kilo. Indeed, I went there many times afterwards, and probably caught all the smaller pike which were hunting in that pool, about five of them. Several times I pulled out the line and found it tangled, the bait fish damaged with the marks of a pike's teeth or missing, but the queen fish still hunted free.

1942

The school term finished, but the freedom of my school holiday was only brief; in two weeks, on 15th July, I started my 'work duty' as a forest worker in Mutenice's forestry department. This work had been procured for me by Tatinek. For the time being I must leave my fishing and painting, but we were hoping that the work in the forest would improve my not very strong lungs which had been affected by pleurisy.

I lodged at the good Srameks with Tatinek, and Mrs Sramek was spoiling me with her cooking even more, if that were possible, than Tatinek. Her food showed no traces of wartime shortages, and she gave us at table the best which she had, so we had for our meals not only rabbits and chickens, but smoked pork too, and even roast duckling or goose preserved in jars since the winter. Such a difference from the Blechas' 'hospitality'!

I was lucky in the forest, too. I was attached to the gamekeeper Fiala, whose son, also called Oldrich and of the same age as me, had been taken away to work in Germany. The Minister of Culture for the Protectorate, Moravec, had given all the young men born in the year 1924 to the Germans to work in the Reich, and Fiala's son had not been able to escape this 'universal duty'. Students, though, were allowed to postpone this enforced support of the Nazi war effort until they had finished their studies. So the gamekeeper Fiala was very friendly towards me, wishing that my lot reflected onto his son, and therefore he eased my labour in the forest as much as he could.

My work started at 8 each morning. We had one

hour's rest at mid-day, when I ate my two slices of bread with lard or some tasty addition from Mrs Sramek, and I finished at 5 in the afternoon when I went to Tatinek at the winery.

For the first few days I was weeding and hoeing round the tree seedlings in the nursery. Later Mr Fiala showed me where the traps for vermin were set on the forest paths, and I should walk these paths, let free the hares or pheasants which were occasionally caught there, and kill the martens or feral cats. The forest was large, and walking along all the paths took up my whole working day. Only once was did I find in the trap a big feral tomcat. He was hissing and spitting like a truly wild beast, and fell to the shotgun of the gamekeeper.

There were some clearings in the forest where potatoes and corn were grown. One day the workwomen who went to hoe the potatoes surprised there a man who was digging out the potatoes with his bare hands and eating them raw. He was only skin and bones, dressed in the remnants of an uniform and when the women gave him a piece of bread he bolted it in a flash. He was a Soviet prisoner of war who had escaped from the transports. Because so many people had seen him, it was impossible to hide him anywhere - in the hysterical aftermath of the Heidrich assassination it meant certain death for anybody who attempted such a thing. The man didn't try to escape any more but let himself be taken to the Directorate of the forest where the German police came for him. I am afraid that the piece of bread was his last meal.

The month of my work duty ended; I returned home, and the two weeks which were left before the end of the school holiday I filled with painting, fishing, and collecting pine cones. That year there was a good crop of them, but they were a long way away and the barrow, on the way home, soon felt very heavy loaded with three big sacks of them so Maminka was glad of my help. They very quickly gave a good heat, and we used them under the big copper cauldron in our bathroom in which we warmed the water for our baths and for washing laundry. It needed only a few shovelfuls of the cones and in no time the water was hot. At the time when the trees were dropping their cones we collected enough to last us the whole year through.

School started again, the last year of my studies - the eighth class. I brought some of my pictures to school from home and hung them in our classroom. That was my first 'exhibition', and it was successful! I soon sold two pictures, one of them to Dana and the second to our classmaster, Prof. Dr. Zurek. Out of twenty which I had painted during the past year, I sold half so I was encouraged to continue with my work.

In the school election I was again elected as the class representative. One day a letter was delivered to me in school. It was addressed to 'The Representative of the 8th A class of Realne Gymnasium in Straznice', and when I opened the letter and read it I was staggered by what it said.

The anonymous writer was appealing to me to

organise an anti-German resistance group and to make connection with a similar group established at the Gymnasium in Hodonin, from which I could collect explosives. After that was a brief description of the objectives of their programme - the destruction of railways, bridges, killing of German guards and so on.

I said nothing to anybody about the letter, not wanting to involve anyone else in this matter. That night I could not sleep and lay thinking what I should do about it. It seemed to me highly improbable that anyone could try to create an illegal organisation just through a piece of paper. What would happen if the 'Representative' of our class had been somebody who sympathised with the Germans? Such a dangerous thing could clearly only be organised through personal contact, without any witnesses and without any incriminating material. It could be the work of a provocateur - and in any case it was deadly dangerous to the eighth class of the Gymnasium in Hodonin where, the writer said, such a group was already established. Information like that in the hands of the Gestapo would certainly mean a raid on the school, probably its closure, and without doubt the arrest and death of the students and possibly other people too. I knew that I had to get rid of such dangerous material in the shortest possible time. If it was meant as a provocation, I could be arrested myself. It would be the end of my quiet days if I didn't hand the paper over to the Gestapo and therefore was shielding enemies of the Reich as clearly indicated by its contents.

So the next day, before lessons started, I waited in the

corridor of our school for our class master and gave him the letter to read. He concluded immediately that it was highly suspicious and decided that I should destroy the missive at once, tell nobody about it and if somebody was searching for it I should deny that I had ever received it. And so I directed my next steps towards the lavatory, where I burned the envelope and its contents and flushed the ashes away. The water removed the heavy burden which had lain on me for 24 hours, but for a long time afterwards I was expecting that suddenly the door of our classroom would open and there would appear the Gestapo. Happily, though, there were no consequences to this nightmare.

Winter that year came unusually early. Already by the end of November the country was covered with freezing snow, but the road to Straznice was cleared regularly by a snowplough, so I could continue to travel to school on my bicycle.

Our class again organised a singing-party for the Saturday before St. Nicholas. We knew that after Christmas there would be the 'coal holiday' once more, in May we would be graduating, and after that we would be scattered to all corners of the Reich. Who knew if we would ever again meet at such a happy communal amusement?

Fera, as before, booked the room for us. This time it was the empty cellar of a small soda water factory in a garden surrounded by a wire fence, so we knew that there we would not be disturbing anybody, nor would anybody disturb us.

I told Maminka that she should not wait up for me, that I would be coming back only late in the night. For safety, so that I could see my way home, I fixed an acetylene lamp onto the handlebar of my bike, electric batteries already having been unobtainable for a long time.

That afternoon I helped carry some benches, chairs and tables from the main building of the factory into the cellar, and a stove to warm the frozen room sufficiently for us to be able to sit there. The stove was of cast iron, already old and with one of its three legs missing, but we propped it up on a brick and it stood quite well. It was then necessary to join together about six pieces of tubing to lead the smoke from the stove to the chimney. The tubes were of differing diameters, so they were difficult to connect and we had to hang them with wires from hooks nailed into the ceiling. After many attempts I managed this job successfully, and we could light the fire in the stove. But the stove had no draught, and the cellar immediately filled with thick black smoke, so I had to separate the tubes again from the chimney, and light some sheets of newspaper inside the chimney itself. That helped. The stove caught the draught and the wood in it burnt well. We had to ventilate the cellar thoroughly, but getting rid of the smoke got rid of the slight warmth too. Then somebody brought a sack of coal on a sledge, so the stove soon radiated a good warmth. We managed everything just in time. Our first classfellows started to arrive about 6 o'clock.

Once again we had invited our classmaster Prof. Zurek and the teacher of Czech language, Prof. Huska. This time they were even accompanied by their wives. Everybody brought whatever he could to eat, the girls had done some baking at home for the party, but to buy wine we had pooled our money - it was better that way than mixing several kinds of wine brought from our different sources.

One song followed another, and there were dozens of them because the rule was that if the song had once been sung it could not be repeated.

After some time I went outside for a 'breather'. Coming back I saw Zorka in the dark corridor leading to the cellar, silhouetted in the light of the open door. We met halfway, I embraced her and kissed her. Clearly I was so brave thanks only to the few glasses of wine which I had drunk. Zorka knew that it was me, but did not protest. After four years of admiration I had shown her at last that she was much more for me than just a classmate! Our embrace lasted only a few seconds. The door to the cellar opened again, somebody was coming.

I returned to the others with a beating heart. I was so happy that I couldn't even sing away my happiness. I started to dance the 'Odzemek', Milan accompanied me with his 'Verbunk'. He was waving his hands above his head, thumping, jumping and twirling. With one of his twirls he kicked into the brick supporting the stove, the brick flew to one side, the stove fell and pulled down with it the tubes for the smoke which had been fixed with such difficulty. I was just underneath them. One of them knocked me on the head, I felt a burning heat at the back of my neck, and the cellar began to fill with a cloud of suffocating smoke.

The singing stopped at once and changed to coughing, panic ensued, all were running from the cellar. Milan, Fera and I stayed. With the aid of newspapers in our hands we first lifted the glowing stove and supported it again with the brick. Our attempt to refit the tubes was not successful, they were too smooth and were slipping on the newspapers. Thick smoke was pouring from the stove, dimming the light of the single light bulb and stinging our eyes so much that we could hardly see, and everybody got in each other's way. It was clear that we could not stay there any longer, so I threw away the newspapers and with my bare hands, luckily hardened by work, managed to join the tubes together in a few seconds. I already knew how because in the afternoon I had been struggling with them for half an hour or more.

At last the stove caught the draught once more. We ran out of the cellar, half suffocated, and left the door open. Thick smoke rolled up from the corridor, and under it there flowed into the room a stream of fresh, icy cold air, so that in fifteen minutes we were able to come back, but the entertainment had been more than a little spoiled.

Zdena did not feel well and wanted to go home. Perhaps she had had a glass too much of the wine, or possibly the smoke had affected her. Zdenek, her beau, wanted to accompany her, but as she was a little unsteady on her legs, he asked me for help. Our journey was considerably prolonged by the parting in front of Zdena's house, and when Zdenek and I came back to the cellar we found the factory gate closed and everything quiet. The company had left and the party was clearly over. What now? My cycle was in the garden behind the cellar, and I had left my mittens and cap in the cellar itself. I was wearing only a thin raincoat, but luckily had my scarf in its pocket. I had thought we would be back quickly after taking Zdena home, and because I had been warmed by the dancing and the struggle with the stove, I had not dressed properly.

But the worst was the bicycle. How would I get back to Bzenec without it? If I was not home by morning, my parents would be worried; Maminka did not like my school parties too much anyway, but I had convinced her that, as class representative, I had to be present. So I took off my raincoat so that I would not tear it, climbed over the wire fence which was two metres high and crowned with three strands of barbed wire, and jumped down into the garden. The cellar, with my cap and mittens inside, was locked, the cycle standing beside the appletree as I had left it. I brought the cycle to the fence and tried to lift it over to Zdenek. It was too high, the handles, saddle and pedals were catching on the barbed wires - but at last and with difficulty we managed somehow.

I climbed back over the fence onto the street. Just as I put on my raincoat we heard behind us "HALT! HALT!". It was a German patrol. A beam of electric light flashed on us, but Zdenek was already running and he vanished round the corner of the nearest small street.

Jumping onto the bicycle, I stood on the pedals and, zig-zagging, fled into the next narrow street.

The clatter of running German high boots faded and was left far behind me.

I cycled through the streets of the town. It was totally blacked out, without the smallest light anywhere, there was no moon in the sky, just the stars twinkling above me. It was difficult to see my way. Only when I was out of the town did I stop. I wound my scarf round my head as a makeshift turban, and tried to light my acetylene lamp, but it was not possible to turn the screw which controlled the water supply - the water had frozen.

So I must manage without the lamp. I could hardly see the silhouettes of the trees beside the road, and was really only guessing where the road was. I kept on course mostly through my ears - the hard packed snow in the middle of the road was crunching under my wheels, the loose snow on the sides only rustled. Even so I had to go slowly so that I would not end up in the ditch. In the forest in front of the bridge over the river Morava it was so dark that I had to get off my cycle and walk with it to that I would not make a mistake and fall into the water. There was such a strong current in the river that there was ice only alongside the banks.

Finally I reached home safely, put my cycle quietly away in the verandah, and at last went to bed.

In the morning I went into the kitchen to wash, and in the meantime Maminka went to tidy my bed. She came back at once, ashen faced, and asked what had happened to me, saying that the bed was in such terrible condition. I went back to my room, with my eyes still half closed, but when I saw the bed they nearly popped out of my head! The sheets and eiderdown were covered with blood and black smudges. I quickly realised what had happened. The black smudges were of the soot which had fallen behind my neck when the smoke tube knocked me on the head in the cellar. One end of it had remained hanging on the wire and all its contents had fallen out of the other end straight down the neck of my shirt, which was as black at the back as if it had been painted. No wonder that I had felt burning at the back of my neck at that moment! There was plenty of the soot to mark my pyjamas and the bedding too.

The blood was from my wrists which I had torn on the barbed wire while lifting the cycle over the fence. There was an especially nasty wound on my left wrist, the left sleeve of my raincoat was all bloody and there were trails of blood on the tail of my coat and on my left boot. My hands were marked even more; the skin on my palms was burned white by the hot tubes, and under the skin were two or three large blisters. There were also deep punctures made by the barbed wire when I had been climbing over the fence. I had blisters on some of my fingers, too, and the backs of my hands were netted with bleeding fissures from the frost. The thermometer had reached -24C that night, even the lobe of my right ear was frostbitten, my scarf probably having slipped off it.

My acetylene lamp felt the cold, too. Its water tank was cracked, and the lamp, therefore, ruined.

That was the end of our party. It seemed that for the sweetness of one kiss I had had to pay very dearly.

On the Monday I went to school again, in other gloves and another cap. Zdenek had the old ones which he had found on the Sunday when tidying the cellar. Cycling was for me now most uncomfortable; the burns on my hand were very sensitive, so that I had to steer with alternate hands.

At Christmas we had a very small fir tree decorated with white chains of meringues on threads. Under it I put my picture 'Fog' which I had painted in the Autumn for Tatinek and which he liked so much. To Stana I gave a portrait of himself which I had painted from a photograph, and to me he gave a most beautiful gift - a fishing rod for spinning, and a 'Hudson' fixed-spool reel made by the Czech firm Stiburek. The rod was 220 cms long, in two parts, of which the lower with a cork handle was of ash, and the other from ordinary 'tonkin' bamboo. It seemed to me so beautiful that I could not tear my eyes away from it and in the evening I put it beside my bed so that I would have it near me.

I don't remember now what other gifts I received, but at that time I could little guess how very much pleasure that rod would bring me in the future - I made full use of it only four years later.

1943

Winter - Matriculation - The orfe - Meander - "Dropping Cliff" - Forest worker - Student again - Gigantic pike II

We named this winter 'the Stalingrad winter'. Even with us the frosts reached -30 C, whilst on the German/Soviet front they were still more cruel. The German troops were not equipped for such arctic conditions, nor were they properly armed, while the new Soviet armies were formed and trained in Siberia, so that they hit the Germans with an irresistible force. They were able to lift the siege of Leningrad, which had lasted for 16 months, during which time 200,000 defendants were killed in the ruins of the city, and another 630,000 inhabitants died of starvation and cold.

The Nazis suffered a dreadful defeat at Stalingrad, where the Soviets captured 91,000 soldiers and 25 generals - including the Commander-in-Chief, General Paulus.

This war on the Russian front at last changed the hitherto unstoppable Nazi progress eastwards, and the Soviet army now commenced on a crushing offensive. At last we felt there was a real basis for the revival of our hopes that Hitler would be defeated and we would once more be free!

During the winter school was closed again, and in March I once more had to spend some time in bed, with pleurisy. When I had recovered our class asked me to make the 'tableaux' - boards with our photographs - for the occasion of our graduation and leaving school. The first 'tableau' was official and I glued our portraits, made by a professional photographer, on a piece of prepared plywood with a heading; the second was humorous - photographs of our heads were mounted on my painting of a Greek battleship sailing the stormy waters between Scylla and Charybdis - the dangerous cliffs of the final school exams.

We were preparing for the ending of our studies - matriculation. A small group of us, after school lessons, would meet in Pruzek's mill where we revised the more difficult lessons. It seemed to me that the more I learnt, the less I remembered. Mathematics and french composition were complete horrors for me. Through my illness in maths I had lost the continuity of the rules of higher mathematics, and in french I had big gaps too. Our french teacher, Prof. Balcar, was very nervous, happiest when he was not disturbed by anybody, and when there was quiet in his class. He worked only with the girls who were sitting in the front benches and were always well prepared. I was sitting in the last but one bench, beyond his circle of interest, and I did not try very much to learn anything of my own free will. I was sitting next to Jarin who helped me with the mathematics, and Zorka occasionally smuggled me a 'tape' - a piece of paper which saved me in french composition.

Even today I still sometimes have nightmares that I am sitting hopelessly at the school bench above white pages of an open book, not having any idea what I should write on them.

Another horror was for me the history and geography of the German Reich, the lessons about which were read in german and were absolutely and totally indigestible. We were taught by a very absent minded lady teacher whom we nicknamed 'The Pipina' after King Pipin 'The Short'. I forget what was her real name.

However, I passed my final written examinations with better results than I had expected. For the oral examinations the teachers gave us a list of questions including some on German history from which they would ask us something, and there were far too many of them for me to remember even the fundamental points. So a few of us asked Pipina to tell us which of the questions she would give us in the exam. The good soul Pipina allowed herself to be persuaded, and she told me that my question would be on the first half of the First World War, the years 1914 - 1916. It was a great relief to me, and I spent more time on learning this subject than on any other. In the end the most important dates and the complexities of the War as 'adjusted' and presented by the Nazi 'historians' stuck in my head after all.

My turn for the exams was on Friday 28th May. I was sure that I would pass and would even get over the worst hurdle - the history of the German Reich. When I came to this subject and was sitting by myself at the desk in front of Pipina and the assessor and chairman of the exams, Pipina's question was on the *second* half of the World War, the years 1917 and 1918! She had made a mistake!! All the days of my learning were wasted, and in front of the commission I could not even tell her about the error. I felt dumbfounded and helpless, in my head was a complete vacuum. However, in a few seconds I had a brilliant idea! I started:

"To comprehend the development of the war at the beginning of the year 1917 one must try to understand the previous situation", and I began to talk about the year 1916.

After some introductory sentences the chairman left. Clearly he was content with my knowledge. Pipina interrupted me after a short while - "That is enough, tell us about the development of the second half of the war!" What could I tell her? I could safely say that it had ended in October 1918 and that was about all that I knew. Pipina made every effort to help me, the assessor was reading some documents. The half hour dragged on as if for ever, but at last we reached October 1918 after all and I could leave the classroom. In a few minutes Pipina came out onto the corridor too, reproachfully asking why I had not prepared myself better. I replied that on the basis of her suggestion I had learned about the first half of the war. She was surprised with that, and when I asked if I had passed the examination she said:

"Certainly - we cannot allow such an artist to fail, can we?!"

And so I 'became adult'. On the leaving examination certificate was printed, firstly in German and underneath in Czech, that I could 'be recorded as a regular student at a University or high technical school', even though everybody knew that the first activity of the 'protecting' Nazis after the establishment of the Protectorate on 15th March 1939 had been to close all Czech universities and high schools...

Just before our final examinations there had been delivered to each boy in our class the call to work in the German Reich. We were the unfortunate 'vintage' of 1924 which the Minister of Culture for the Protectorate, Moravec, had given to Hitler as young slaves for his factories, and the Germans wasted no time at all - these were the 'studies at University'! I was ordered to go to some factory at Marklisa in Poland, but first I needed to add to the summons the results of a health examination. At this time Dr Fiala was still living in Straznice, and he did not recommend my 'total work engagement in the Reich'. He asked for my health examination to be undertaken by the German health authorities in Brno, where they agreed with his diagnosis - physical undernourishment, and shadows on the right side of my lungs. They recommended that I should work in the Protectorate. No wonder - although I was 1m 77cms tall, I weighed only 56 kilos, and the defects in my lungs were painful when I undertook any physical exercise.

Tatinek was once again able to arrange work for me in the forests in Mutenice. I was to start work on lst July, and therefore I tried to make the best possible use of every minute of my last free month to paint and fish.

The Spring thaw was especially dramatic this year

because of the unusual and extreme masses of snow which had fallen. Even the relief canal, where during the summer we had fished for burbot, was not able to contain the voluminous waters of the River Morava which overflowed its banks and changed the surrounding meadows into a giant lake. At the point where the Bzenec brook Syrovinka ran into the River Morava, only a few dozen metres from its mouth, the water of the lake breached the banks of the brook and masses of water ran down to join the main river again, flooding the meadows somewhere lower down.

When the spring floods dropped, clean water ran again through the stream Syrovinka, but the River Morava was still muddy. A deep hole had been eroded where the waters had broken through the protective banks of Syrovinka, and I thought that the fish swimming against the current in the Morava would certainly stop in the lagoon there to relax and clean their gills in the clearer and calm water.

On the first day I started to fish there I caught three good tench, and on the next day five, but unfortunately some fishermen, who were hanging around the riverside, saw my catch and next day all the possible places around the hole were occupied. There were even two men there with nets, trying their luck and they were all blessed with at least one good fish - tench, carp, barbel, chub and even small catfish.

When the waters in the Morava had cleaned themselves too, the fish no longer gathered in the hole, and the fishermen stopped fishing there. I liked the place, so when they had gone I tried my luck again. It was possible to come on my bicycle right up to the water, and I was hoping that some larger fish would stray there from the Morava. Most of all I liked sitting above the deepest water where the eroded bank fell straight into the depths so that it was not necessary to cast the line.

I put the float 2 metres from the hook baited with a worm and dropped it down below me, laying the rod by my side so that only its tip showed above the water. Because nothing was happening, I was looking at all sorts of things around me, only not at the float, but when I did at last look at it again, it appeared to have moved about half a metre away, against the current. The water there moved only very slowly, but even so it was not possible that it would flow from the Morava to Syrovinka. I looked again and saw that the float was really moving slowly alongside the bank. But it was not jerking, only drawing away more and more quickly. I struck, and felt a good fish. I could not land it from the high cliff so, carefully releasing some line from the reel, I walked a short way downstream, where I climbed down and nearly fell onto the alluvial sands below the hole. After a great fight I landed the largest tench I had ever caught from the hole, only a fraction smaller than my record from the 'Great Ditch'.

A few days later I caught there a 1 kg orfe *(Leuciscus Idus)*, which fought with strange movements like somersaults. It was a beautiful fish, a relative of chub, with vivid colours and purple fins, shining as if made of polished metal.

With this catch my fishing in the hole had to finish. Huts grew up near the river, a pile driver and a narrow gauge railway with waggons arrived. The damaged bank was strengthened with piles, the wall repaired and the hole filled with earth.

About three hundred steps from the hole which had been formed in Syrovinka by the spring flooding was a remnant of the old bed of the Morava. The river had flowed there in a meander, on the outer edge of which was a fifteen metre high cliff while the inner side was flat and covered with long grass and reeds. It was separated from the main river by the river wall.

The water there was black and treacherous, and below the sandy cliff it was several metres deep. Even in the hottest summers the water was only warm near the surface. Although everybody knew it was so, and also that at least two swimmers were drowned there every five years or so, there were always plenty of people bathing in the lower part of the meander. I did too, and stopped only when the water claimed further victims, two brothers, one who was drowning and the other who was trying to rescue him.

The upper end of the meander belonged to the fishermen. There were large carp there; I would somethimes see a group of them swimming slowly just under the surface, but although I only managed to catch some smaller carp and pike I was always hoping that maybe this time I would be more lucky and hook some really good fish...

I especially liked the steep, high sandy cliff which was there. In full sunlight it radiated with pink, yellow and golden tones standing out in contrast to the dark pinetrees framing it and to the underlining dark surface of the water below. I had wanted for a long time to paint a picture of it, so I went there with my painting things and my fishing tackle too.

First of all I cast my rod for the carp, baiting my hook with a piece of dumpling. Then I erected my easel, put on it my sheet of plywood and started to work. From time to time I glanced at the float, but it didn't move at all. Soon I was so absorbed in my painting that I nearly forgot the rod lying in the grass beside me.

Half an hour passed, and something rustled in the grass. I thought it was a mouse or a vole and didn't pay it any attention. After a moment I heard the rustle again, and this time it lasted longer. A few seconds later I realised, and it flashed across my mind - the rod! I saw it jerk in the grass. The line was stretched, and the float somewhere under the water. I threw my palette and brushes to one side, jumped to the rod, and found the fish had caught itself - who knows when it had eaten the dumpling and the hook?

It was a carp. Playing and landing it was not difficult, but it was not the giant for which I had been hoping, only just under 2 kilos, though it was the largest which I had caught there. The thought that it had caught itself, that I had missed the dramatic moment of its taking the bait, when the float was sinking in the water, took some of the pleasure from the catch.

That was the first and last time when I tried to fish and paint at the same time. The fisherman in me won after catching the carp. Though I caught nothing more, I never finished the picture. It really is not possible to fish and to concentrate on painting, or to paint and to watch the float.

However, both the painting and the fishing had strong influences on me. While wandering round the various waters, I was observing my surroundings more and more, and they pleased me more and more. I realised that the part of Slovakia where fate had blown me was as picturesque as anybody could wish.

I fell in love especially with the meadows, enlivened as they were with the blind arms of the Morava, their groups of alders, willows and poplars, the horizon closed by the line of the White Carpathian mountains and with the high vaulting of the sky above. It was a wide country which seemed to give one free flight in those years without freedom.

At the time of the spring floods the meadows were silvered like a broad lake, with little boats of white seagulls. In summer they waved with juicy grasses and were scented with hay, whilst in autumn they bloomed as far as the eye could see with purple carpets of autumn crocus, and in winter the white covering of snow made the distances seem even greater.

Ancient wooden hay sheds stood there, raised on piles, and there were quiet pools with waterlilies and - I am quite certain - water nymphs and pixies, while at the edges of the grasslands were orchards with old and bent appletrees from which spectres hooted in the night - tawny owls.

I liked the crying of the seagulls, the calling of the lapwings, the songs of the skylarks, the clattering of the storks which nested in the willows, and the hooting of the little owls at eventide.

Any and every way that I turned there was always something which caught my eye and which was worth painting, even when it was only a simple track with a puddle of rainwater and the vaults of heaven above it.

It was a cosy countryside of quietness and peace, with everything in it living in complete harmony.

The 'Dropping Cliff' was a charming part of the untamed Morava river, where a high, almost vertical wall of solid sand, the remains of a prehistoric dune, rose above the quickly running waters. Under a tiara of dark pine trees on its top were many sand-martins' holes drilled into it.

A short distance upstream was a ford with quickly running water in which, as regularly as a pendulum reminding one of time passing, there swung a tree trunk anchored to the bottom by its roots. It sloped downstream, and on the stumps of its branches there clung flags of dry grass, remnants of the last spring floods.

A little higher was a pool with a pleasant sandy beach where we used to swim. In summer the sand on the beach was so hot that it nearly blistered our feet. In this pool an asp was 'beating', hunting so violently that the splashes could be heard even away from the beach.

I had been using my old tackle for fishing in the hole on Syrovinka, but now I thought that the time had come to try my beautiful Christmas gift from Stana - the spinning rod. I had not yet been brave enough to take it to the water. Ever since the first year in Straznice I had been fishing without a licence - during the war the regulations were not so strictly enforced, but what would happen if somebody liked my new rod and wanted to confiscate it? Here very few people came at all, I could learn without interruption how to cast with the, for me, new technique of a reel with a fixed spool. Possibly I might be lucky and catch the asp.

Some years before I had seen how one of the fishermen caught a big asp in the Morava using an artificial lure called a 'Devon'. It was a torpedo-shaped metal fish with pectoral fins like the blades of a propeller. Now I made a sort of 'Devon', too, using a chromed metal pencil guard.

Milan came with me that day to the Morava. He was swimming and sunbathing, I was trying to fish. My casting was not bad, but the 'Devon' was wrongly balanced. The head which I had made of lead was too heavy and flew in front with each cast, and the treble hook at the end of the lure often caught in my line so that my 'Devon' did not rotate properly when I rewound the line.

On the opposite side of the river another asp was

beating; it was bigger than the one I was trying to catch, but I could not yet manage to cast so far. Still I would be happy to catch the smaller fish - it certainly weighed no less than 3 kgs.

My next cast was a good one, the hook did not catch in the line, and on rewinding the line I felt that the lure was rotating well. It ran only two or three metres through the water and then jerked so strongly that the fish nearly wrenched the rod from my hand.

"I have it!" I called to Milan.

The asp ran against the current with such force that I was not able to stop it and had to follow it along the bank. I could see the line going deeper and deeper, and then it snagged on some under water branch. I was at a loss as to what I should do. Never before had I had such a fighting fish on my rod, and I had as yet had no practice with either the rod or the reel. I was so thrilled that my hands and knees were shaking. Suddenly the running fish stopped. When I kept the line taut I felt the fish jerking on the end, but when I loosened it, the line drooped. The fish had knotted the line somewhere down below. What next? I walked down river, pulling the line, but unsuccessfully - it did not come away. I could still feel the fish quite clearly, so the line must have caught on some flexible branch. I tried against the current, but with the same result. Then I calmed down a little.

I gave the rod to Milan who was watching my fight and trying to help with advice.

"Hold this, and I will dive down and possibly free it!"

I say to Milan.

Milan holds the rod, and I, in my underpants, go as far into the water as I can reach, with the line running through my fingers. Then I have to swim slowly.

"Loosen it!" I say. "Now it is right".

Hovering just above the snag I tread water and pull up the line, but that doesn't help. It seems it is deep just here. I kick into some branch - a sunken tree! There remains only one solution - to dive.

I take a deep breath, but my first attempt is not successful. In no time my head is above the water again, and I am spluttering. It is unbelievable how strongly the water is lifting my body!

After a brief rest, I take another deep breath, splash with my legs on the surface of the water, and swim down, hand over hand, along the line. I must use only my legs so as not to break the line with my hands, and the water is almost lifting me again when I hit some branch with my hand and am able to hold onto it. Here is the first loop of the line. I move it off the broken branch and swim lower. Though already short of breath I must still hold it for a few more seconds and pull myself ever deeper. At last I can lean my back against some stump, but the line slips out of my hand. Hurry! - the water is pressing into my ears and my chest is nearly bursting.

I hit my back on something and - am stuck! The realisation goes through me like a knife. Suddenly I cannot hold on to anything, am tossing about, my eyes starting from my head in the dim brownish-green light, and the bubbles are rising from my nose. Through my head flashes a picture of my unhappy Maminka. The pressure in my ears changes to a steady drone - and then I realise that it is the branch on which I am stuck. Being held there by my pants I am hovering above it, so I can reach down to the stump, give a hard jerk - and manage to free myself.

I have to take a breath before reaching the surface of the water, and half drowned I inhale more water than air and start to cough. Milan is swimming not far from me and helps me to the bank. I lie on the sand, shaking, and vomiting the water I have swallowed.

After a long time I get up, pick up my rod and stretch the line with my hand. I can still feel how the fish is waving in the depths and how the twig is bending further and further so that the line hums like a taut wire. At last it slashes the water - broken...

From then until the end of the war I didn't take the new rod in my hand any more, and was fishing only with my old tackle.

June flew by all too quickly. As well as fishing, I painted four more pictures including my own portrait which I thought was especially successful. It was my first portrait painted from a living model - seen in a mirror.

On 1st July I once more joined the Mutenice forestry as a worker. It was good to see the Srameks again, but not so good that the gamekeeper, Fiala, had been moved to another area so this time I was immediately subordinate to the Director, Loffler, which meant the end of my sauntering gently through the forests.

I started the job by having to load dry oak bark into roofed railway waggons. The bark was used for tanning leather, and was in one metre long pieces, just as they were stripped from the trunks. The bark was brought from the forest to the railway station on horse drawn carts, and I was made to load the bark onto the highest part, under the roofs of the waggons, where nobody else wanted to go.

The sun was burning without mercy, making the roof of the waggon as hot as an oven. I, close to it, had to push the bark as far inside as I could manage. It was difficult to move around in there and, in the darkened interiors with my eyes full of dust, I could hardly see anything, while from the rear another worker, standing comfortably, kept handing me more and more pieces. The sweat poured from me, the bark scraped my knees and elbows and, like a file, rasped the skin from the backs of my hands and fingers. My trousers suffered badly, too. I felt much as I had done in my work at harvest time last year with Blecha, only this time I had also to listen to more and more taunts of "This is the real leaving examination!", or "This is a different sort of Latin!", or "This is better than sitting at a bench and learning nonsenses." Because I was so thin it was always I who had to finish the loading, under the roof, but I was too proud to complain.

At the end of the second week, the Director called for me and gave me easier work in his office. From the overseers' books I rewrote onto account sheets the hours worked by the women hoers, treecutters, waggoners bringing the wood and bark, and assistant workers. From charts I calculated the wages due, which, for the treecutters were partially substituted with offcuts - the branches and tops of the felled trees. As the overseers only brought their books to the office on Fridays at midday, and the workers were paid on Saturdays, I had to toil over the papers even until nine or ten at night, which was for me still worse than loading the bark.

At the beginning of the next week I was put to hoeing with the women, and weeding round the seedlings in the forest nursery. To be bent over a hoe for a full day might be held to be easy work, but I was the only man there amongst a dozen women, and they regaled me with jokes with double meanings which I did not understand. I didn't know how to respond to them, and so I, through keeping silent, had to put up with much laughter. Perhaps it was not really as bad as I felt it to be - the women were simply amusing themselves at my expense - but for me it was deeply wounding.

On the Friday I was once more working until late into the night on the week's accounts, and on the following Monday again in the nursery. In the middle of that week I had to work on the monthly balances, which would not come right. I had to count and recount, again and again, and each time the result was wrong. Next day I was still sitting over it, but with the same result. In the end the Director discovered that I had written the dates from two books on one person's name. Over a hundred workers were employed in the forest, often several members of the same family in different jobs, differently paid, and I had written two people with the same name in one column. Of course I could not know as much as did the Director or the overseers about their employees.

At last the first month ended, but I was not looking towards the future with much enthusiasm. Perhaps modelling in the pottery would be better. At least there I would not be laughed at, my work would be appreciated, and certainly I would have some spare time for fishing and painting. What a pity that I had not known that the gamekeeper, Fiala, had been moved!

The following week the Director wanted to teach me how to deal with the stock books. Clearly he wanted me to have an official position there, but I hated the paper work, and at last we came to the agreement that I would undertake only the weekly and monthly accounts. After all, my pay was for the lowest category of assistant worker. A qualified accountant, to whose work mine was equivalent, would have been paid a much higher salary. I preferred to load the bark onto the horse waggons in the forest with the other workers; it was much better than sweating in the railwaggons. I would work in the office only on Fridays.

The next week was the pleasantest I had had in the forest. I was, with one of the overseers, numbering the 'rounds' of wood piled in cubic metres. I carried a box in which was 'the hammer', a die with four rings of numbers from zero to nine, black shoe polish with a brush, another set of larger numbers with red colour, and an ordinary heavy hammer. The box was quite heavy, but it had a strap so that I could carry it over my shoulder.

We walked along the forest paths and tracks beside which were piled, between pairs of stakes, the wood from treetrunks cut into 1 metre lengths. The overseer would set the appropriate number on the die, blacken it with the polish and, with one swing as if with a hammer, stamp the number onto the white cut end of the largest log in the pile. He would then write the number into his book, and we would go on to the next 'metre' or 'double metre'. The longer pieces of wood, the whole trunks, were numbered with the red numbers.

A week later, though, I accompanied one young foreman to mark the trees which were to be felled. He gave me a large bucket of thick limewash in one hand and a big brush in the other, and we went to a specified section of the forest which was to be thinned. It was in a damp dell overgrown with nettles and blackberries and infested with mosquitoes, so that even in the hottest summer I had to wear a jacket - my immunity to mosquito bites having diminished somewhat since leaving Straznice. The sweat was pouring from me, the nettles were stinging even through my trousers which were nearly in holes over my knees after being rubbed by the oak bark I had been loading, and I could not drive away the mosquitoes from my face and neck because both my hands were occupied. The young chap was only showing me the chosen trees and I marked them with a cross at shoulder height with the limewash. I soon learned which of the trees had not developed properly or had been overgrown by the surrounding trees, and this helped me in my work and saved me from unnecessary walking. It was terribly tiring, my legs were twisting and catching in the dead nettle stalks from last year, which in places were lying like tough ropes. Even worse were the blackberry stems. The 10 litre bucket full of lime, which is much heavier than water, seemed to me to get heavier and heavier even when the contents were diminishing, and after two or three hours I could hardly carry it. I started to feel my elbow, which I had broken in my childhood but which had caused me no trouble for several years now. I felt how streams of sweat were running down my back and, pouring from my forehead, were making my eyes sting, and I suffered from terrible thirst. But I didn't give in. In the afternoon I took less limewash in my bucket, and left my jacket in the hunting cabin - the biting of mosquitoes was more bearable than the heat.

Three days passed in this way. On the Thursday morning there was already such a sweltering heat that I could scarcely totter with the bucket. That afternoon there came a thunderstorm. In the heavy rain, dressed only in my shirt, I was soaked through in no time at all. The water poured through my shirt and trousers so that not one dry thread was left on me. The temperature dropped so much in the hail which followed that I was shaking with the cold. Marking the trees was finished. We went back to the cabin for my jacket, while the rain continued, sloshing even into my boots. My companion who, before the storm, had only been carrying his jacket over one shoulder now at last showed some feeling for me and took the bucket and brush from me. His suit of loden cloth and high rubber boots had protected him from the rain.

Half an hour passed before we reached the hut, and it was still so cold that even in my dry jacket I was shivering and my teeth were chattering. I said that I was finished with work for today, and went to Tatinek in his office. It took me 45 minutes to get there, and I arrived still soaked through. When Ing.Vobr saw me in this condition he gave me two glasses of brandy to drink, after which I at last felt warmer, and he brought me a dry shirt, trousers, and jacket of his own into which I changed. By evening I felt unwell - possibly it was partly the brandy which I had never drunk before.

I felt no better next day, and would not have been much use in the forest, so I went with Tatinek to his office from where he rang to the forestry department that I could not come. I was so glad - I did not have to undertake the weekly accounts!

On Saturday we went home by train. I was shaking with fever. In the middle of the summer I had to stay in bed with another pulmonary inflammation. This time even the local doctor concluded that that meant the end of my 'total work duty', and that if I wanted to recover physically I should stay at home. On the basis of his health report I was released from both the forestry work and the 'total work duty'.

During the time I was working in the forest I had

arranged with our immediate neighbour, the tailor Stanek, to have Tatinek's old loden coat, from which he had already made my warm mittens which I used when cycling to school, remade for me into a three-quarters 'hunter's' coat. This had a half belt at the back, two lines of bone buttons down the front, a pair of large pockets at the sides, and another pair on the chest. The lining was made from a white sheet as we did not have any better material to use. The coat had epaulettes and green velvet facings, and I bought a green hat to go with it. At the time when the tailor was making my coat he asked me if I would be interested in 'underground' work. I didn't understand the question. I thought he wanted to offer me some work digging a cellar. He explained that he meant activity in the local undercover anti-German group.

I told him I would not be very useful to them because I was working through the whole week in Mutenice, and came to Bzenec only at the weekends. He asked if either Tatinek or Stana would be interested in joining them, but I gave him the same answer. Clearly that was sufficient for him. He only told me that I should not talk about the conversation either at home or anywhere else.

My work in the forest ended before my coat was finished, but because I was ill after coming back from Mutenice, the tailor probably thought I would not be a very good partisan anyway, and he did not mention the matter any further.

By the Autumn I was fishing and painting in my 'new' coat, and even later it was my favourite and the most useful item in my wardrobe.

After consultation at home, Tatinek arranged for me to be entered as a student at the local wine school, in that same school at which he himself and my godfather, Uncle Slavek, had been studying.

It is true that I had been relieved of my 'work duty' as a result of illness, but some of the local people could be upset that at the time when their sons had to be working in the Reich I was at home and spending my free time painting and fishing. Students were exempted from working in the Reich, and so it would be more tactful, and safer, if I too became a student. So once more I started to walk to school.

Because, thanks to Tatinek's profession, I already had some knowledge of the main subject, viti-culture, I was accepted straight into the second year, but being still ill had to miss the beginning of the school year. I was older than most of the students, and in answer to the professors' questions said that after the war I wanted to follow in Tatinek's footsteps and to study at the University agricultural school. It was the simplest explanation.

In the lessons of viti-culture, the growing of grape vines, and in the production and treatment of wine I already knew more than even the advanced students, as I did also in Czech language, chemistry and mathematics, which at the wine school were on a more simple level than they had been at the Gymnasium. So I was lucky in not having to study at all. At last I could use the information I had learned at the Gymnasium and especially from that which I had absorbed without realising it from Tatinek's vast knowledge during all the past years.

We were taught Czech and maths by Prof. Hosek who, in the first week, invited me to his house to help him correct the Czech compositions of my schoolmates. This task was repeated regularly almost every week, and for it, each teatime, I earned a bread roll and a cup of cocoa, which I had last drunk before the war. After some time our teacher of fruit growing, Prof. Kostiha, asked me to help him in the preparation of his book which he wanted to publish, so I was working for him too. He lived not far from us, and from other materials I was re-drawing plans of shrub and flower gardens onto uniform sheets of paper. I spent many, many afternoons there, and there too I always had my afternoon tea. To make my work more interesting and to stimulate my own creative powers, from time to time I would draw my own designs for such gardens.

Of course I still had my own homework for school to write as well, and so the school took a surprising amount of my time. I could paint only rarely, and hardly managed to fish even at weekends.

If the weather was good I went with Tatinek to the pool with the pike queen. I was sure that even though the meadows had been under water at the time of the Spring floods the pike would still be in the pool. We were fishing with our old rods, and in case the pike might perhaps bite on a worm again, I fixed my hooks on a steel line trace.

The pike didn't bite, nor did the smaller fish, the steel line was too hard and the usual fish were discouraged by it, so after some time I returned to my original way of fixing the hooks on a normal monofilament line.

This year the fishing was not so good there, so I crossed the water to the other side. A little higher upstream it was easy to jump across where only a narrow stream ran through the deposits lying on the river bed. I was hoping that, at the other side of the pool, I would catch some small rudd with which I could bait the pike line.

The bank there was covered with shrubby willows, but in front of them was a clearing where, not far from the bank, some sunken branches stuck out from the water. Between the land and the brushwood there should be some small fish.

I was using only small compost worms, but nothing happened. The float seemed to be asleep. During at least two hours I caught only one tiny fish which had swallowed the hook too deeply. I baited the pike line with it, but it was probably dead already. I thought it was better to leave it where it was, and look at it again only when I had caught another bait fish.

At last the float moves. It jumps nearer to the sunken branch and sinks about two inches below the surface of the water where it sticks and stands without any movement. Probably it was some small perch which, pricked by the hook, has pulled the hook under the branch and then swum away. I must look and see if the worm is still there. I pull. It is surprisingly heavy, but the weight is rising slowly. Then, all of a sudden, above the water appears a gigantic head not a full yard from me and I see the half open jaws of the pike, between which could easily vanish a chub of a kilo or more. It is she! For a second time she has taken the worm! The first time it had at least been a good garden one, but now it was only a miserable little compost worm! The head vanishes with a loud splash, and I am left looking at the bitten off end of my line. What kind of a pike is it that is eating worms and ignoring the bait fish on my other line, or at best only tearing at it and leaving it? I am sorry that I was not fishing with the steel line trace, but now it wouldn't help any more. After all I was fishing for bait fish only with my ash rod without a reel, and I could never play such a giant on such light tackle. She would break either the line or the rod.

I am astonished that I could lift so large a fish above the level of the water without any resistance. Possibly she had been so surprised that she had not realised what had happened to her.

I invented systems of single-, double- and treble-hooks from which, I liked to imagine, not one pike could ever escape, but to 'my' fish all these clever snares were only for ridicule.

I rode there each free Saturday and Sunday, but all my attempts were unsuccessful. The pike ignored me till late Autumn, then ice and snow covered the water and that was the end of my fishing. No matter! I would come for her again in the Spring!

During 1943 we had been greatly encouraged when we heard how the German forces had been withdrawn from North Africa 'for tactical reasons', and that the Italian fascist forces had surrendered to the Allies. The Germans still held most of Italy, including Rome, but the Russians were pushing the German forces in the Ukraine back to the west too, and we began to believe that the final defeat of the Nazis was now only a question of time.

1944

Miluska - Stana's love - Water maiden - Giant pike III - Photographer - Food supply - Foreshadowing of the end - Long haul flyers - Bomb attack

Dancing lessons were organised in the school, so once again it was possible to dance as much as I liked. Straight away I was attracted by a smallish, dark-haired girl called Miluska; she danced well and evoked in me a wave of feelings and hopes. Soon I arranged a rendezvous with her, and afterwards we walked together, usually in the woods behind the railway station. We met at least once a week. I looked forward so much to each meeting with her and when I saw her, looking so pretty in her soft fur coat, my heart began to race. I felt great tenderness towards Miluska and wrote poems for her, was deeply in love and very happy.

I liked so much to walk hand in hand with Miluska, and my courage grew so that I even kissed her sometimes, very tenderly. At last I had my girl, my true love, as I had dreamed about since childhood. My feelings were so strong that I started to think about marrying.

Once I spoke about it with Maminka, and to my surprise she didn't laugh at me. She liked Miluska too, knowing her from church services on Sundays, but she suggested - wisely - that the occasional selling of my pictures would not be sufficient to support a family, and that as after the war I wanted to go to University it would be more sensible to wait to see how my love developed. Maminka told me that she knew there were other admirers too, but I was so much in love that I did not want to believe it, even when on several occasions I saw in front of Miluska's house other boys who were clearly waiting for her. One day though when we had arranged a bicycle trip together, arriving at the square to meet her and seeing there already four or five young men with their bicycles with 'my' girl, I apologised that I could not go with them and returned home.

Miluska was so pretty that it was natural she should have many admirers and that she was pleased by that, but I was deeply wounded. I did not want to be just one of her entourage, I could not share her with others who were clearly more amusing than I - still a shy and diffident dreamer. So I parted with her. No, I was not jealous, just sorry that she was not able to choose, that she didn't want to be only with me as I wished to be only with her. It was a pity. She was my first real girlfriend and true love!

Even Stana's love for Liba burned itself out; she had found more satisfaction in the company of another girl. But Stana soon recovered from this shock. He met Olga, at his office, and he was in love again. She had a twin sister Jirina, and they were two years younger than Stana.

One Sunday morning the twins came to visit us. Stana wanted to introduce his Olga to us and Jirina came with her. All four of us went for a walk in the Castle park - I walking with Jirina - while Maminka stayed at home preparing a very special lunch.

Lunch was ready when we came back from the walk. We sat around the table in our kitchen, having no diningroom in the house. It was a hot summer's day, the window was open to the garden and on the table was Maminka's best tablecloth - the silk one. Tatinek was sitting at the head, at the sides were Stana and I, each with a girl on our right, and Maminka was serving the soup. It was my favourite - vegetable soup with young carrots, parsley root cut in small pieces, cauliflower florets and young peas, all boiled in stock made from rabbit bones. We said grace and started to eat.

At that moment I heard a buzzing. Through the window flew two struggling flies, passing close by my ear. In their struggle they flew straight into Stana's soup plate. What then happened in one second I see still today as in a slow motion film. Stana glances hurriedly at Jirina sitting on the opposite side of the table, and in the following moment is pressing one of the flies into his soup. The other fly he is lifting with the soup in his spoon, bringing it to his mouth. He holds the mouthful momentarily as he makes up his mind and then, with one big gulp, swallows the soup, fly and all. The girls didn't notice anything. The second fly vanished the same way - unseen!

After the first course followed rabbit schnitzels with our young potatoes and lettuce, and lastly an excellent strawberry tart sprinkled with a sweet, crunchy crumble - everything, of course, being home produced. We all, including Stana, enjoyed the meal.

That evening we accompanied the girls to the railway station and put them on the train which would take them home. When the train started to move away, puffing loudly, I could not contain our secret any longer and exploded into a spluttering laugh. Stana explained:

"But what could I do? Certainly on their first visit to us I could not let them think there were so many flies in our house that they were falling into our soup!" So Stana bravely saved our family's reputation.

Instead of walking with Miluska I started painting again, and later fishing too.

A little further than the canal where with Tatinek we had fished with our bare hands for the burbots there was in the distance a line of poplars through the meadows on the left of the road. I thought that there could be water below them, and as it was nearer to home than the pool with the pike queen I would go and look there. From the main road I rode over a small bridge onto a track, raised a little above the meadows beside it, which led me almost to the edge of the water. I disturbed a couple of lapwings, calling "pee - wit!" and swooping close beside me. They must have had their nest somewhere nearby.

The water was really beautiful. On the opposite bank it was shaded by poplars, elders and an ancient willow on which, quite certainly, in the light of the full moon used to sit the 'vodnik' - the 'water sprite'.

The nearside bank was lined with giant mare's tails and yellow irises. Most of the water's surface was covered by the leaves of white and yellow flowered water lilies, and one could clearly hear the smacking noise made by the tench nibbling under them. Some of the leaves were even moving with their nudging, as if they were being touched by the fingers of some water maiden, but sadly it was not possible to fish there. Any fish I caught I would lose in the jungle of water lilies. But at least I could paint the scene, and so I went there again the very next day.

It was a sweltering afternoon, not one leaf moved. I became absorbed in my painting and at first didn't hear the rumbling of thunder in the distance. When I realised that the storm was nearing, I packed my painting as quickly as possible and cycled back to the road. In the meantime the sun disappeared behind a thick black cloud, and the first heavy drops of rain began to fall. I jumped from my bicycle, laying it on the bank beside the road and, pushing my picture, box of paints, easel and stool in front of me, crawled underneath the little bridge.

This little 'bridge' was in fact only a short tunnel under the track which would lead the water from the meadows if they were flooded. It was made from a few concrete tubes about four feet in diameter, but they gave good dry cover even though I had to crouch to be able to sit there. I did not think the storm would last very long.

The first drops changed into a steady drumming, broken by fresh thunder. Towards the last murmuring of it, something rustled at the side of the road, and into my hiding place crawled a breathless girl, or young woman, about 20 years old. She was not surprised to see me, having seen my bicycle outside. She had come there on a bicycle too. To make more room for her, I moved closer to my picture. After a few words about the painting and the storm we fell silent.

She sat close beside me, her white blouse stuck to her body by the rain and showing her breasts heaving with her deep breathing, her pale green skirt slipped from her bent legs and unveiled her rounded knees, her wet and golden hair, from which the rainwater dripped, was warm and sweetly scented. At a sudden flash of lightning accompanied by a deafening clap of thunder she instinctively pressed closer to me with her hip and shoulder. I felt chilly and dizzy, as if in our touching there streamed between us something of the electrical tension in the atmosphere - the sweltering heat, her female scent, her white knees, full rounded breasts, and fine blushing profile - I wanted to lift my arms and really press her close to me. My heart was beating somewhere in my throat, I felt faint and tried to move aside a little but there was no room because of all my painting equipment. I could only lean away from her shoulder and close my eyes so that I would not see the white knees, but it was as if they burned me even through my closed eyelids. I stretched again, and pressed against her hip and shoulder once more. She must have felt me start to tremble but she didn't move away.

And so we sat there, huddled up together, without speaking, I full of confusion and desire, she radiating sweetness and captivating temptation.

It was only a shower. The humming of the rain stopped, the thunder died away and we sat there, as if captured by the tubes and our feelings. Perhaps we were both waiting for the first move to be made by the other. Then she stirred. I felt as if some link was breaking between us, as if I was awaking from a dream.

Once outside, she was looking at my picture.

"I will finish it tomorrow. The grass is soaked with the rain and I do not want to splash through it."

"How old are you?" she asks.

"Twenty", I reply.

"I thought that you are much, much younger!" she says with surprise.

She helped me to lift my box of paints and the picture onto my back, I fix the easel on the crossbar of the cycle, and put the stool over the handlebar. We both push our cycles onto the road, from which steam rises in the sunshine.

We are standing one in front of the other. She is looking deep into my eyes, and I again feel that I am about to swoon, as if I am falling into the blue-green pools of her eyes.

It lasted perhaps three or four seconds. Then she smiled, moved a tress of wet hair away from her forehead, and said:

"Anyhow, you are a child." She turned quickly, got onto her bicycle and in the mists rode off in the direction of the town, Veseli. Above her arched a rainbow.

She didn't look back. Still elated I started to ride

home - in the opposite direction.

Next afternoon I went to finish the painting, half expecting that at any moment the vegetation around the pond would part, and that from the water would emerge a watermaiden with a water lily in her soaking golden hair, of which a tress had slipped onto her forehead. She would be wearing a translucent pale green skirt, through which would shine her white knees...

But the water remained closed - with seven locks...

I left the water with its lilies to the water sprites, and on Sundays I often went to the pool with the pike queen. My third year there already! There were substantially fewer fishes in the pool, the queen having eaten them, but she always ignored any small fish with which I baited my line.

One day I tried to catch some small rudd as bait, fishing to the right of the drowned brushwood where I had last seen the pike. Once again she took the small worm on my hook, scarcely five feet from the bank, but this time, after her bite, I didn't manage to lift her head. She reacted to my pulling by diving down to the bottom of the water, and showing only her tail as wide as two hands. At that moment she cut the line with her razor sharp teeth, the tail sank, and to the surface was washed up a swirl of mud and half rotten leaves which had fallen into the water last autumn from the willows beside the pool.

That was the last time I met the pike queen - though I heard about her once more, when the war had just ended and I was working with others on clearing the debris from the bridge on the 'Northern' railway line which had been demolished by the Germans during their retreat. One of the men there was talking about how he had been fishing with some Russian soldiers on the blind arms of the river Morava, using hand grenades to catch the fish. It was a cruel but simple and successful method. They threw the grenade into the pool and the fish, killed or stunned by the explosion, rose to the surface. Sometimes there were so many fish that the top of the water was white with them. They took only the biggest, catching them in a landing net on a long pole. The largest fish of them all was a gigantic pike from the pool at 'The Wattle'. She weighed 23 kgs!

That was the sad end of my pike queen. After my last meeting with her and having lost any hope of catching her, I spent most of my free time in painting. The best of my pictures I had framed, and the owner of the workshop exhibited them in his shop window. Amongst them was a small picture of the birch wood behind the railway station where I had often walked with Miluska. Even though I never met her now, I missed her and the picture reminded me of her. Several people wanted to buy it, but I could not bring myself to part with it.

I finished my schooling with excellent marks, and was asked to make the graduating 'tableaux' for our classes. When collecting the photographs for it I met the local photographer, Mr Vratislavsky, who offered to take photographs of my 'Birches', and of my other pictures too. With our first few words we discovered that we both 'liked' the Nazis to the same degree, and of course we were talking about the successes of the Soviet armies on the eastern front. Mr Vratislavsky had very accurate news not only of the situation on the Russian front but also about the battles in the Mediterranean and Atlantic and the war between the Americans and the Japanese in the Pacific.

Later on at his studio I met with another 'rebel' and then with the source of his information, a Czech ex-general, now retired. He had an excellent radio and listened regularly to Radio Free Europe, broadcast from London, even though he knew from the printed card which must be attached to all radios that 'Listening to foreign broadcasting is punished by arrest or even death'. Only after the end of the war did I learn that General Koutny was the Commander of the underground 'Army of the People', to which were subordinate all the groups of partisans in our district.

Our meetings at Mr Vratislavsky's became more or less regular. We met at least once a week, and the news from London which was at last very encouraging became for us, as well as for many other Czechs, an important moral support.

The Soviets were forcing Hitler's army back to the west, the British had achieved overwhelming supremacy in the air and were bombing Germany's industrial centres and even Berlin, and in June came the 'D-day' invasion of

France by British, American and Canadian forces, which proved to be the greatest technical operation in the whole history of war.

The Germans responded to the invasion by bombing London with Hitler's 'secret' weapons - the flying bombs with jet engines, the 'V1's which, launched from the Dutch coast were really devastatingly effective, but neither they nor the later 'V2' rocket bombs changed the course of the war. To all of us it was now clear that the fall of the Nazi regime was inevitable.

This showed drastically in our supplies of goods which became more and more limited, and our weekly food rations were now restricted to the absolute minimum necessary to sustain life. Milled beans were added to flour, and to the bought bread probably something even worse - it was dark brown and sticky. There were warnings broadcast on the radio and in the newspapers against eating the bread when it was fresh because it was not safe. We should eat it only when it was at least three days old. By then it was already hard, and therefore nobody would eat too much of it. The ration of meat for a week was scarcely enough for one small portion, and the only fat - very poor quality margarine - vanished completely. As a substitute for it there was a small amount of 'artificial honey' which was supposed to give us the essential calories necessary for life. Instead of eggs we had a yellow powder which contained no nourishment at all, it only coloured the dough slightly yellow 'as with real eggs'. People said that it was produced from cocks' eggs! Milk was blueish water without any trace of cream, and there was so little of it that we bought it only once a week so that we were able to bring 'something' home in the bottom of our milk jar. Luckily we were also still able to buy the excellent milk from the Jureckas.

Coupons for textiles were allotted only for babies' nappies, and to newly married couples for them to buy the most fundamental items of bedclothing. Now was even abolished the entitlement coupon for one bicycle tyre every two years which had previously been allowed for those people who needed bicycles in order to get to work or school. There was no other way than to patch the holes in my tyres with pieces of still older tyres. The tubes, which were already just one patch beside another, I repaired with glue which I made from my tennis shoes which I had had and been using since 1936 (for some reason my feet were not growing much), and which, after all the years of use, had come to the end of their life. Their soles were made of raw rubber, and I dissolved bits of them in benzene to make the necessary glue.

Leaving the Gymnasium meant the end of obtaining the occasional extra bit of lard which my classmate Mirek had sold to me, his father being a butcher. Luckily just at the right time Stana managed to find assistance for us. He was overseeing two building sites in Breclava where his firm was building a furniture factory and the railway points centre. Some workers from Slovenia who were employed there smuggled in cigarettes, tobacco, meat and lard from home where supplies were not so drastically restricted.

Breclava was outside the Protectorate, in the previous borderlands occupied by the Germans in 1938 as the so-called 'Sudetenland', and therefore was now part of the German Reich. Smuggling over the State frontier was difficult. Even in the Protectorate itself there were German controls on all railway stations opening not only suspicious looking baggage and suitcases, but also ordinary shopping bags. They were confiscating any 'black' goods, but somehow Stana managed very successfully.

Now the events of the war began to roll like an avalanche.

On 1st August started the uprising of the people of Warsaw against their Nazi occupiers. This time it was not just a specific group, as it had been at the time of the ghetto uprising, but a manifestation representing all the peoples of Poland. They, and we with them, were hoping that the Russians would break through and join the uprising but, even though the Soviet army was so near Warsaw, they turned to the South and left the desperate city to her own fate - to her destruction.

On 15th August Rumania, until now an ally of the Germans, capitulated. Two weeks later the Soviet troops invaded Bulgaria.

Then in Slovakia the Slovak patriots, on 21st August, encouraged by the approach of the Soviet army, proclaimed the establishment of the new Czechoslovak Republic and started an armed uprising against the Nazis. This was bloodily suppressed by the Germans, and the remaining scattered groups of resistance fighters ruthlessly liquidated, while more than 60 small villages in which lived people who had helped the partisans were burned to the ground and their inhabitants murdered. In the village of Kremnicka alone 747 people were massacred.

At the same time, on the western front, the Allies continued to make progress. Paris was liberated on 25th August, Brussels on 3rd and Antwerp on 4th September. On the southern front, in Italy, the Germans were forced to give ground to the Americans who, from the Italian airfields, attacked targets in countries occupied by the Germans north of the Alps.

It was just before noon when I heard above the forest the approaching hum of aeroplane engines. The sound was somehow different to that to which I had become accustomed, but in that instant it was drowned by a dry, sharp rattle lasting only two or three seconds. The echo had not yet died when it was covered by a further 'trrr...', followed by a sharp hiss of steam. I ran to the attic and looked through the open window. I just managed to see two aeroplanes disappearing high in the sky. Above the forest a white cloud of steam was rising. They had got it! Another steam locomotive pulling a train loaded with 'materials important for the war' had been destroyed, and the traffic on the Northern railway, the important link between the Adriatic and the Baltic through Vienna, Moravia and Poland, would be stopped at least for some time. This line used to carry dozens of trains every day, usually with more than a hundred waggons each, so blocking the line in this way with an immovable train was extremely effective.

In the afternoon I went on my cycle to look at the train. Already other curious onlookers were there, pointing out one rail which had been shot through by a bullet as if it had been made of cheese. They dug out some of the bullets from the sand beside the railway. Burning coal fell from the engine, and some of the front waggons and sleepers were burning too. Two boys had picked up some empty shells they had found deeper in the forest.

The next day being a Saturday Tatinek had come home from Mutenice, and in the afternoon we went to look at the train again. Railway workers were dismantling it, and a small locomotive was pulling parts of the train back to Breclava where there was an important rail junction. The damaged engine, burnt waggons and half of the train still stood on the rails.

Then we went into the forest to look for any fungi which might be growing. Far away from the railway line we found a shell from a heavy half inch calibre machine gun, then a second and a third, so we started to hunt for them instead of fungi. We also found the steel links which had originally joined the ammunition together in a cartridge belt. Surprisingly the shells were of brass; the Germans had been making them from steel for a long time already and varnishing them so that they would not rust, being so very short of copper and zinc for manufacturing brass.

We found over a hundred of the shells with their links. How was it possible to fire so much ammunition in such a short time? I joined all the shells and their links into two belts - one would have been too heavy to carry - and put them over the handlebars of our cycles. We then walked our bicycles back through the forest. At that moment I noticed some coloured paper on the ground. Printed on it was CHEWING GUM. At this time I had no idea what it could be, but it must have been dropped from one of the aeroplanes.

At home we put the belts of shells in our attic. Such beautiful brass - it could be useful sometime in the future.

Several days passed before even the destroyed locomotive was moved away and the rails and burnt sleepers were changed. Surely the Nazis were missing the held-up trains very badly.

The 'long haul flyers' were not the only American aeroplanes with which we met. Soon we saw hundreds of them, whole swarms coming from the south, and their humming sounded like the music of paradise to our ears. Certainly that *must* already mean the defeat of the Germans!

Often in the sky one could see formations of white lines, with sometimes a darker spot in front, or a bright spark - the reflection of sunlight on the bombers. The formations were flying to the factories in Poland; luckily they only passed over us. I could not help thinking about the factory in Marklisa where I should have been working.

Behind the first formation of American bombers which passed over our heads we saw something falling which sparkled as it fell. We found they were strips of aluminium foil which the aeroplanes dropped to confuse the German radar stations, and we collected them from our garden, the street and even the forest, putting them into a box to use as decorations for our Christmas tree! No Christmas decorations had been for sale during the war, so they would be added to Maminka's meringues.

As well as the American bombers, we saw huge German planes carrying the name 'Gigant'. They were real monsters, with ten engines along their wings and about twenty wheels in two lines under their fuselage. They flew with deafening thunder, so low and so slowly that we could clearly see the ribbing of corrugated aluminium sheets covering the planes. So overloaded were they that they could hardly stay in the air. The Germans were transporting whole factories in them, somewhere to the North, from endangered places in North Italy and Austria.

Twice we heard distant rumbles. We were told that the Americans were bombing Viener Neustadt.

About noon on 20th November we heard the rumbling again, but this time it didn't stop. On the contrary the sound increased until it reached such an intensity that our windows rattled. It was somewhere near us.

Stana later wrote about it:

"It was a fateful day. At that time I had one lodging room in a family house in Hodonin *(the town in which he was working)*, and another in Breclava in a cottage owned by an old woman. In Breclava I had one office in a wooden shed, and a second in a room of the old railway points house on the line to Vienna. As well as overseeing the building of the new points house, I was looking after the building of a furniture factory for Mr Vaculik.

"The attack by the American 'Flying Fortress' bombers came on that day from the south: Klagenfurth, Vienna, Viener Neustadt, Breclava, Hodonin, Zlin, and everything happened around noon. The railway station in Breclava was bombed. The wooden shed and the old points house where I had my offices were destroyed, also the post office and the whole track system of the station. During the bombing I was standing near Mr Vaculik on the as yet unfinished third floor of his new building. The centre of the town was in flames, the church and the Gestapo headquarters on the main square received direct hits. A splinter of a bomb fell right beside me. I wanted to pick it up, but it was too hot.

"From Breclava I started to walk to Hodonin along the railway line. Later I was able to get onto an emergency train - a locomotive with one goods waggon - which got us to the town only at night (it is 23 kms from Breclava to Hodonin). Walking through the streets was very difficult in total darkness, there were bombcraters and electric wires down everywhere. My landlord was in hospital, wounded by a flying splinter, and my bed was covered in debris. But somehow I managed to sleep a little in it, and in the morning I set out on foot to go the nearly 20 kms to Bzenec.

"I don't know how many died in Breclava. In Hodonin there were over 300 deaths. I realised then that everyone has his own candle - be he old or young ... Possibly that is a bit fatalistic, but it is so.

"When I was in Breclava, standing on the unfinished building, I was watching the German fighters attacking the bombers. Part of the town was burning. I saw one member of a bomber crew quietly floating down on his parachute, but all at once the parachute seemed to stick in the air and the man was falling helplessly down, shot from his harness. His candle, too, was blown out ..."

The day after Stana's return we both went by bicycle back to Hodonin. There was complete devastation in the town. One bomb had exploded in the vicinity of Stana's lodging, and the house where the Studenkas lived was damaged too, its windows were without glass, the doors whipped out of their frames by the force of the explosions, the walls cracked and the plasters fallen off.

While we were helping to pack some of the twins' most necessary clothing into two suitcases a timebomb exploded somewhere nearby, which half deafened me, and more plaster fell from the ceiling. I looked out of the window, and saw only a column of yellow-brown smoke. On our way home we saw several people beside a ruined building - they had found a woman who had one of her legs trapped under some stone steps which had collapsed.

We learned later that they were able to save her, but only after amputating her leg.

We got back to Bzenec with the girls and the suitcases, and Stana and I gave up our room to them. For the time being Stana then had to sleep on the bench in our kitchen, and I in the cellar where Stana helped me make an emergency bunk.

I think the girls returned to Hodonin only after about a month because it was not possible to live in their house which was so damaged and without windows and doors. Even before this bombing there had been a great shortage of glass, and now it was necessary to repair thousands of buildings and reglaze thousands of windows.

Maminka was not very thrilled with our enforced visitors, not because she was niggardly with hospitality, but she was upset that the girls never offered at least to wash the dishes after meals, nor to help with the cooking or even tidy the room in which they were sleeping. Stana's first love, Liba, had been quite different and was well educated in work around the house. So Maminka worried about Stana's future.

After the bombing of Breclava and Hodonin the defeats of the Nazis came in a torrent.

On 6th September Bulgaria asked for an armistice, and then declared war on Germany.

The Soviets continued to make progress on the southern flank of their front. They went into Hungary, and on 15th October Hungary asked for an armistice. The Germans still held Budapest, but their position on the Eastern front was clearly collapsing.

On 16th December the Nazis organised their last great offensive action, this time on the Western front, where they attacked the Allies in the Ardennes. The radio was once more playing victory fanfares and promising that the German armies would soon sweep the rest of the plutocrats into the ocean. The Germans sent there all the best units which they were able to muster, the mobile forces, tanks and well trained S.S., complemented by their last reserves - superannuated veterans and youths of 16. They managed to hold on in the forests, and to stem the progress of the British, American and Canadian armies. The Nazis knew that a retreat from the Ardennes would mean transferring the land battles onto German territory, and after that there could only follow their complete defeat.

On 20th December the Soviets encircled Budapest.

Now we really believed that this would be our last wartime Christmas, that the end of Hitler's 'Thousand Year Reich' was nearing, that his forces would be completely defeated and that we would once again be able to breathe freely and without fear. On our Christmas tree glittered the aluminium foil strips which the American bombers had dropped to us.

1945

The front approaches - Partisans - Battle of Bzenec - Liberated! - Snipers and mines - Journey to Prague - Examinations for entrance to the Academy

The Soviet armies progressed invincibly to the west. They were already fighting in both Poland and Slovakia, and at the end of March the deep rumble of guns came near to Bzenec and German units were passing through the town. It was forbidden to go out of the house after dark, but all the same in the dusk everybody was digging in his garden, hiding stores of food for worse times to come. We, too, filled a five litre demijohn with flour, pressed down well with a wooden stick and corked. The cork we protected with melted wax. Maminka melted nearly all our reserves of fat and poured it into two wine bottles, which we corked well too, and filled a jar with preserved minced goose meat. We buried them all at the end of our garden, covering them with a piece of sacking and earth.

For several nights we heard flying over us single Soviet aeroplanes, their slowly vibrating engines making a quite different sound to the hum of the German planes. People said that they were dropping partisans behind the German lines. In the distance we heard the 'tatatat' sounds of the heavy machineguns, and from the window in our attic at night I could see in the western sky the lines of shining bullets marking the fighting aeroplanes.

During the night of 4th/5th April loud detonations rumbled from the south. The Soviet planes were bombing Hodonin, the town which had previously been so damaged by American bombers. What had happened to Stana who was working there?

The belts of empty machinegun shells which we had picked up in the forest were right beside the window in our attic, and Maminka didn't like having them there in full view. She told me I should throw them away somewhere because they would only bring us trouble.

Now, when everywhere around us were swarms of German soldiers and the S.S. Command's headquarters was established in Mr Skala's villa opposite our house, it was completely impossible to take the belts out onto the street. So I buried half of them in the hay which was stored in the attic, and the other half I dropped down the well in our cellar. Only two shells, for which we had not found the links, remained on the windowsill.

On Friday 6th April Tatinek returned home from Mutenice and Stana from Hodonin, both of them having survived the bombing all right.

At the time there were so many German soldiers in and around Bzenec that there was no room for them in their barracks, and so we were forced to have billeted on us some higher officer and his orderly. We could offer to the officer only Stana's ottoman in our room on which to sleep. Stana moved at night onto the padded bench in the kitchen. The orderly stretched his canvas and blanket on the floor in the hall. The officer said that Maminka should not make up the bed, he wanted to remain dressed and would only take off his boots and relax. The door to the street remained unlocked. In front of it stood a guard.

The officer hardly touched his meal which the orderly brought him from the army kitchen, and he was very apologetic that he was disturbing us. He said that he was doing his duty in the front line because he believed that by so doing he was fighting against communism. He told us he fully realised Germany's present situation and knew that we were longing for the arrival of the Russian army, but that once we really knew what communism meant we would be cured of our illusions. He said that now we were certain that the danger of communism was only a product of German propaganda in which we did not believe, but that the Soviet Union was *really* one great prison in which the people were governed by fear, where each person was watched by somebody else. All soldiers were watched by the army police who shot those who hesitated even slightly during the attacks, so that the Soviet soldiers had no other possibility than to go forwards under all conditions and their losses were unimaginably high. If we thought that the Soviets would bring freedom to us, we would soon recognise that under their supremacy freedom did not exist.

That evening we thought that the officer's view about the Soviets was dictated to him so that we would be more afraid of the future than of the past six years of German rule which we had all experienced. We knew only too well that, under their so-called 'protection', we had lost our freedom and felt as if we were in a prison, the Nazis had closed our universities and forced our people into slavery in the Reich, they were arresting, torturing and killing our intelligentsia and thousands of innocent people. We knew that our previously rich country had been plundered, we were afraid of the Gestapo and their collaborators and, after Heydrich's assassination, we knew the rabidity of the Nazis with their executions on such a massive scale that they were beyond even the most horrific imagining.

The officer stayed with us just a few days, coming and going only at night, so we hardly saw him and never talked with him again, but later how many times I had cause to remember his words!

The officer left, the guard in front of our door vanished and we could lock the house again.

On Sunday morning, 15th April, we went as usual to church. Only Stana stayed at home. He did not feel well and he had some work from his office to do, so he was sitting at home over his drawing board.

When we were returning home from the church after the service and were nearing the end of the town where we lived somebody stopped us and warned us that we should go no further. The Germans were there, catching partisans, and that they already had Stana. We thought that possibly the Russians had dropped some partisans during the night from aeroplanes. The remark about Stana seemed to us nonsensical. It is true that earlier we had heard some shooting, but we wanted to go home and so we continued on our way.

At the entry to our little street was a group of S.S. men, and on the stairs of the house of the tailor Stanek, at the corner of our street, there ran a stream of blood. The S.S. stopped us, but when we said that we were coming home from church and when we showed them where we lived they let us go through. At home we found Stana, very pale, and with his left cheek red and swollen. We asked him what had happened.

Stana told us briefly that, not long after we had left, two people had run through our garden, below the kitchen window. Zolina was barking wildly at them and clearly attacking the two men. As nobody should have been in our garden Stana went to see what was happening there. The two men, who were in civilian clothes, kicked out at Zolina, driving her back into her kennel and, with pistols in their hands, forced Stana to climb over the fence to the Staneks' yard, following behind him. In the yard were some S.S. men who were, clearly, interrogating Mrs Stanek, but as she knew no German she could not understand what they wanted. They were asking for some 'hole', Stana translated for her, but she didn't know what they meant. When Stana said that they were probably asking for the cellar, she exclaimed "Jesus Maria!" and led them to the cellar.

Then the two men were leading Stana across the road towards the lower part of our town. When, in a narrow street, they were passing the yards of some cottages, Stana jumped over one of the wooden fences, hoping that he would be able to escape somewhere behind it. The men started to shoot after him, the bullets whistled around his head but not one hit him. He managed to reach the end of the yard in only a few bounds, and pressed himself into a recess to hide, but there was no possibility of escaping from there. A guard dog started to attack him, and the Gestapo reached him easily. One of them struck Stana across his cheek, and they led him, with his arms raised, to a cottage where they were already questioning some other people. They were searching for partisans, but Stana didn't know anything about them. He explained that he came only for the weekends, that he was working in Hodonin, and that he had tried to escape because he thought that they wanted to kill him even though they had no reason to do so, and so on. After the examination they let him go home.

Scarcely half an hour had passed when there came a ring at our doorbell, and an S.S. officer with two soldiers pushed their way in, forcing us with their bayonneted rifles into the kitchen. There the officer was asking us questions about the partisans and each of us must show our passport, the 'Kennkarte'. From these he could see that Tatinek and Stana were employed away from Bzenec. He then asked us if we knew where our neighbour, Stanek, could be, but we didn't know anything about him. Then they started to search throughout the house, looking in wardrobes and under beds, and we had to go with them into the attic. They immediately noticed the two shells lying on the windowsill and asked us where we had the machinegun, but we explained how we had found them. Then the soldiers searched for some time through the hay with their bayonets. By great good fortune the belt of the shells did not rattle.

We went back into the kitchen. The men asked for a candle, and were pushing us in front of them into the cellar. Tatinek was paler than I had ever seen him, completely ashen faced. There was electric light in all rooms in the cellar, so they had no need of the candle. In the fuel room there was now only a small pile of coal - we had wanted to buy a load in the summer again - and three sacks of pine cones. They shook the cones from the sacks, looking for something, but of course found nothing else inside. Then they moved the larger pieces of lignite from the heap of coal, but nothing was hidden under them either. Finally they lit the candle, moved off the concrete cover of the well and, by the light of the candle, were looking inside. Even there they did not find anything. The belt of shells was under water at the bottom, the surface of the water probably reflected the flickering candlelight and so they didn't notice anything foreign there. I felt the weight lift from my heart. What would have happened if they had found the shells in the hay or in the well - how could I have explained why I had hidden them?

Again and again they were asking where we thought that our neighbour, Stanek, could be, but we were only surprised that he was not at home.

Only when the S.S. men had left could we breathe more quietly. Tatinek was so pale because he had thought they wanted to shoot us in the cellar. It would not have been the first case of 'mistakes' by the Gestapo or the S.S.

Later we learned that our street was full of partisans,

but that the organiser of the partisan movement, Stanek, had managed to escape. So that was the 'underground work' that he had been offering to me!

That evening, from the Hohns' cottage further up our street, we heard the desperate lamentations of Mrs Hohn, and later through the quiet of the night there rang out one shot from the garden of the Skalas' villa opposite us. Next day we learned that the S.S. men had been examining and torturing and then had shot dead Mr Hohn, who had been hiding 14 Soviet partisans at home. All of them had managed to escape from the S.S. raid except one whom the Germans had shot and killed as he was running away.

On the Monday morning the Gestapo and S.S. units disappeared, taking with them two of our citizens - Mr Juriga and Mr Jelinek. Mrs Stanek had already been taken by them the day before. The pool of blood on the Staneks' stairs was the result of her examination by the Gestapo. They had beaten her so vehemently that they had broken her teeth and her face. Poor Mrs Stanek - how could she know that her husband was hidden in the attic of the house of Professor Kostiha in the main street, only two blocks away, nearer to the centre of the town? I would not be at all surprised if she had not known anything about the partisans. She never spoke too much. She left two children - a girl of about four and a boy about two years old.

That Monday, 16th, the Germans prohibited us from leaving our houses. Everybody going into the street would be shot and killed. All windows had to be closed.

From the east we heard the barking of machineguns. Over our heads shells whistled and exploded behind the Pisek sugar factory. The Germans had fortified the factory, and they were directing their fire towards the Soviet positions concentrated near the factory. During the day the noise of the battle increased from time to time, but later it dropped once again. At dusk it reached such an intensity that we were expecting the Soviets to break through, but when darkness fell the firing stopped except for the sporadic sounds of a machinegun or a lone shot.

Next day, 17th April, the Germans were still holding the sugar factory. It was a complex of the tallest buildings in the area, standing on a small elevation, so a good view could be had from it. The Soviets were responding to the shelling only with light weapons. The whistling of shells above our heads and their explosions behind the factory continued throughout the day with increasing ferocity and came nearer. Some shells exploded so close to us that our house was shaking, so I left off my observation of the factory from the window in our attic and we all went down to our cellar. For some hours Stana and I played chess. Maminka was the first to leave. She went up to the kitchen to cook lunch. Then Tatinek followed, and only when Stana and I had finished our game did we follow too, although the cellar was unpleasantly cold. We went on playing chess in the kitchen, not being able to do anything except wait for the battle to be over, and so we shortened our time.

In the afternoon I started to draw pencil portraits of Tatinek and Maminka, the first time that I had drawn from live models other than myself.

Judging by the noise which reached us, the Soviets attacked again in the afternoon, but once again they were repulsed. Shooting continued into the night, but the shelling stopped.

18th April, but the sugar factory still did not fall, and the fighting continued. The noise of the guns was so close that the attacking Soviets could only be a few hundred metres beyond the Skalas' garden which screened the view along the road to the factory so that we could not see what was happening there. We could hear though that whatever it was was very close. Bullets were whistling through the air and machineguns were firing from the top of the hills planted with vineyards which rose above and behind the garden. But even this time the Soviets did not manage to get through to us.

To the noise of the battle were added new, sharp detonations. The Soviets were shelling the factory with 'Katusa' rockets, of which the Germans were very much afraid. From our attic window I could even see some of the flashes of their shining white explosions. The factory was burning.

At 11.30, just before noon, we heard a loud detonation. The Germans had demolished the little church called 'The Old Castle' which stood on top of the hills overlooking the town, and also their lookout post from which they had been directing their gunfire. Later in the afternoon another loud detonation shook our whole house, and the glass nearly fell out of the windows. In front of the sugar factory there rose a yellow-brown column of smoke - the Germans had demolished the railway bridge where the line crossed with that going to Veseli, and also a smaller bridge on the Veseli line near Bzenec. They had then poured paraffin over the freight train that was standing on the track and set fire to it.

As darkness fell we saw some people running over the fields to the train. The bent figures were removing something red from the one wagon which remained after the fire. Then came the sound of machinegun fire, the figures fell to the ground, but after a while they were running away again. Looting from the wagon continued into the night.

During the night we heard heavy traffic on the road - cars, lorries and tracked vehicles were passing by. The firing stopped, and before morning the traffic stopped too.

On Thursday 19th April we awoke to an unusually quiet day, interrupted only by an occasional single shot.

Around 10.00 o'clock we saw the first non-German armoured person, a man dressed in civilian clothes - a green hunting coat - with a small rucksack on his back and a rifle in his hands. He took shelter behind Stanek's house, that being the first house on our side of the road leading into the town. I ran out to greet him. He was asking "Where are the Germans?" I learned that he was from Prague and that during the hunt after Heydrich's assassination the Nazi's had murdered the whole of his family. He had managed to escape to Slovakia, and since the time had been taking revenge on the Germans, hunting and shooting them as wild animals. Now he was in the Soviets' front line so that he could win the highest number of 'trophies'. He did not stay long.

Soon afterwards I saw the first Soviet soldier - a Rumanian - and behind him a handful of other Rumanians. All of them were taking cover behind the houses and running, bent double, along the ditch beside the main street which was at right angles to the narrow streets opening onto the vineyards. From the vineyards came the thuds of sporadic firing from the German snipers who were still on top of the nearby hills.

Later we heard other explosions, the Soviets blowing up the anti-tank mines laid by the Germans on the Pisek road.

Behind the first group of Rumanian foot soldiers there followed, on GAZ lorries, the other units of the Russian command.

WE WERE FREE !!

It was 19th April 1945.

Now I could understand why the battle of the sugar factory had taken so many days. There were no heavy weapons in the column, nor any tanks, only a few anti-tank guns which looked more like children's toys, four 12 cms calibre mortars, and one lorry carrying the 'Katusa' rockets.

Our house was pockmarked with the shells which had fallen so near that the plasters had been cut through to the underlying brickwork, and steel splinters with edges sharp as knives were lying on the ground. We took some of them as souvenirs.

The looting of the train continued throughout the whole day, and later we learned that the 'red' which people were carrying were German supply parachutes - not long afterwards many Bzenec inhabitants were wearing red shirts and blouses - and buckets and sacks filled with sunflower seeds. Part of the load in the wagon was burnt and still smouldering, but there was still plenty left on which to feed rabbits and poultry.

Then for the first time we saw, near the train, our neighbour the tailor Stanek, who had escaped the raid by the Gestapo just in time and since then had been hiding. A pretty widow in his workshop had taken care of his two small children.

We had been liberated, but the war was not yet over for us. The German snipers, dug in behind the vineyards on the hills above the town, were shooting at the Rumanian soldiers walking on the main road or on the field tracks below the vineyards, but the Soviet commander took no action to wipe out the snipers.

On 25th April a Rumanian soldier tried to reach the

Germans, but he did not even get half way there when there was an explosion. Only when the cloud of smoke had lifted did we see the soldier half sitting, holding the stump of one leg which had been broken off below his knee. The other leg was without a foot. Land mines! The wounded man was shouting desperately for help, but nobody wanted to go into the minefield. His voice became weaker, now calling only at intervals on his mother and on Christ. It was painful just to listen to it. People were standing right by the vineyards but did nothing. At last Mirek, who lived opposite us in the villa housing the S.S. command post, brought a short ladder and went with Stana for the soldier. They were both as yet without families, so "it would not be such a loss if they died", said some of the onlookers.

They brought the wounded soldier back safely. He was only a boy, 17 or 18 years old, and was still conscious. Round the blackened stump of his leg, from which a white bone stood out, he was tightly holding a strip of cloth from his trousers, trying to stop the bleeding, but the foot was missing from his other leg too. His face was as pale as death, only his hands were red with his own blood. Somebody gave him a cup of water to drink. Stana became a hero in my eyes.

Now it was clear to us why the Germans, before their retreat, had prohibited us from leaving our houses. They had been fortifying their sniper positions, and planting mines in the vineyards below them.

These totally unorganised 'advances' continued throughout the following days, too. All the soldiers who tried to reach the German snipers were wounded by the mines. One of them avoided all the mines but was killed, almost at the top, by a hand grenade thrown from a German fox hole. Once two soldiers fell, one who trod on the mine and the other who tried to rescue him carrying him from the vineyard on his back. Another soldier was wounded in the stomach by a sniper, so high up the slope that it would have been total suicide to try to save him. The Germans had the target in front of them as if on a plate. The wounded man was laying there for several hours, calling at first for help and then on the Germans to finish him. His voice became weaker and weaker, and he died at nightfall. Not one of those who had been wounded in the minefield survived. Even when they were brought out they died later at the army surgery.

Some of our people went to the Soviet command and asked them to finish off the German snipers, either by bombing or by shelling. Under the fire of the Germans it was not possible to clean the vineyards of the mines, and people were dying needlessly through bullets or explosives. After several days they achieved their objective and, in the lower part of our end of the town, Olsovec, a heavy mortar was brought into a firing position. The soldiers fired a few shots, with the sole result that the Germans responded by firing back at them with a light mortar. Neither side hit their target. The German scattered their fire along the main road, but they didn't find the Soviet position which was hidden behind the houses.

Because of all this we had been without bread - a vital part of our food - for several days. Maminka had been making our own bread throughout the war, but to bake it she had been taking the dough in its straw basket to the baker in town. Now it was impossible to go to the town as the road was in the line of fire from the snipers. On the open places where the road was not sheltered behind the houses it would not be possible to run whilst holding the bread dough in our arms.

Now, though, when we heard that the baker in town was already baking bread again, and from better flour than previously, I decided that I would go into town and bring some home.

In the morning it was still cold, and so I put on my 'hunter's ' jacket. In case the snipers mistook my jacket for a uniform it seemed safer to walk in the ditch alongside the road. When I came to the part opposite the nearest street, where there was open space, I crouched down low, walking upright again only when I was behind the houses once more. Then, at one instant, came the already familiar sound of the German mortar being fired, a metal 'plonk' ringing out, so I was prepared for it and was already lying in the ditch when the shell exploded near me. I felt deaf from the explosion, I was spattered with soil and grass, and could smell burning. It must have been very close. Getting up from the ditch I saw, only 10 or 15 metres away, a cloud of smoke rising from the field, but not very clearly. My glasses! The right side of the frame was broken and the glass in pieces. I must have ploughed the bottom of the ditch with my head! I put the damaged frame in my pocket, and continued on my way to the town, although my left ear was still half deafened.

I managed to buy the bread, and to return home without further accident. Only when I was cleaning my jacket did I find in the back of it, where it must have lifted when I fell into the bottom of the ditch, two small holes. A splinter from the shell had flown right through it.

It was not possible to repair the damaged spectacles, nor to buy a new pair at the opticians, so I had to adapt to being without glasses and since that time have no longer worn them. I could not see quite so well into the distance, but that was perhaps better for my painting.

The German snipers stayed holed up for eleven days. When we expressed surprise that the Soviet soldiers allowed themselves to be shot like rabbits, we always heard the same reply "Eto nicevo - nas mnogo!" - That's nothing - we are many! Others will come behind us. The life of one or a dozen, or even a hundred or thousand, is not important - Nas mnogo! And so the sniping also died away, because at the end the snipers had no more food, water or ammunition so, on 30th April, those who survived were pulled from their holes - like rabbits.

56 Rumanian soldiers fell in the battle for the town, many of them through the mines and sniper fire.

The shooting by the snipers had ended, but the danger of the landmines lasted longer, as a dreadful threat to anyone who entered the vineyards. None of those unhappy people wounded by the mines survived - not only the soldiers, but also those working in their own vineyards, and even the expert who was searching for the mines. Nearly every day we heard explosions from the vineyards. Twenty two inhabitants from Bzenec were killed by the mines, and a further 172 died in the concentration camps.

At the headquarters of the S.S. in Kyjov were discovered the dead bodies of Mrs Stanek and two of the partisans, Mr Juriga and Mr Jelinek. Through what dreadful tortures they must have gone before they were relieved by death. They all had crushed fingers, feet burned with boiling water, and their bodies mutilated by wounds and bruises.

The Nazis were really inhuman sadists, even at the time when they must have seen already that they had lost the war and known that soon they themselves would be sitting in a courtroom.

Russians succeeded the Rumanians. The soldiers were established in the town barracks, but some of them were billeted in private houses as well. Sergeant Kozuskov lodged with us. He had been an orchard keeper on a 'kolchoz' (a collective farm) in Georgia, and Tatinek was able to speak Russian with him, remembering the time when he had been a prisoner of war in the Ukraine. Through their conversations the sergeant learned that I was a 'chudoznik' - artist.

Next day some officer came for me and I had to follow him to the barracks. There I was asked to help with the decorations for the celebrations on 1st May. I should write about twenty slogans in cyrillic from the samples which were given to me - 'Da Zdravstvujet Krasnaja Armija' - Long Live the Red Army - , and 'Za Stalina, Za Rodinu' - For Stalin and Country - and so on. They gave me a big room in which to work, and all the necessary paper, canvas, paints and brushes. The carpenters made the stretchers for me, and I was given a pass enabling me to go in and out of the barracks at any time. I was also allocated a soldier as assistant; he helped me stretch the canvasses, and I started to work, writing the slogans on dozens and dozens of metres of paper and canvas, and painting two big portraits of Stalin and Lenin. My assistant brought me excellent meals from the officers' canteen, and by the evening before 1st May I had managed to finish everything that had been planned. The barracks were decorated with my slogans, and Stalin and Lenin looked down from the walls in the big hall. The commander of the garrison was so content with my work that he invited me to the festive luncheon. I said that I would like to bring Tatinek with me too because he spoke Russian, so we were both of us invited.

There were lots of official speeches before the meal, one following another. Of course I understood nothing of it, except the closing phrases 'Da Zdravstvujet ...', and when the commander thanked me.

The food, when it came, was so rich that it surpassed all expectations. Many toasts were proclaimed - to Stalin, to the country, to peace - I tried the vodka and sweet wine, groups of soldiers were playing concertinas and singing...

We went home only in the late afternoon, and I felt the wines.

We dug our reserves of food out of the garden. It was no longer necessary to hide them.

On 30th April Hitler committed suicide. On 2nd May the Soviets entered Berlin. Germany was defeated.

On 8th May Germany capitulated. It was the end of the war. In Prague, however, the Germans only laid down their arms one day later on 9th May with the arrival of the Soviet tanks.

In May we started to pack up our books, crockery and other small things as we were to return to Znojmo. Tatinek was transferred back to the research station there so that he could continue with his work of breeding vines which had been interrupted by the war. This time he was to be the Director of the station. Ing. Vobr was transferred from Mutenice to Bohemia.

At that time I was working with other people on the demolished railway bridge; that was when I heard about the sad end of my 'pike queen'.

For travellers to be able to continue on their way, they had to change trains near the ruins of the bridge. I was always asking the people passing by if amongst them was somebody from Prague. One day I was lucky, and in answer to my questions the man told me that the entrance examinations for the Academy of Fine Arts would be starting the very next week. He said that the railway lines to Prague were still broken in some places, and it was necessary to change trains as here so he did not know how much time I would need for the journey.

I didn't know anybody in Prague, but the photographer Mr Vratislavsky had a colleague there, Mr Krejci, and gave me his address together with a letter in which he asked Mr Krejci to help me by allowing me to stay with him for a few nights.

I packed up a few of my paintings and drawings, and in a small suitcase some clothing and necessities and, being afraid that I might miss the start of the entrance exams which began on Monday 11th June, I got on the train already on the Saturday, 9th June.

Tatinek accompanied me to the station. We went early, when it was still dark. The trains had only just started to run again, there were not many of them, and they kept to no timetable. One simply had to wait until a train came.

The train arrived about 4 a.m., so packed with people that it was impossible to get in through the door. So I passed my suitcase and bundle of pictures through the open window and then, with Tatinek's help in lifting me and that of the passengers who were pulling me, I managed to squeeze inside. I asked for my suitcase and my pictures, and was told that they were safely with the other baggage at the end of the corridor, having been transported there above the heads of the standing passengers. I parted from Tatinek with a look, and the train moved off.

It was an ordinary train, stopping at each station and sometimes between stations too. It often had to go slowly over newly built temporary bridges or parts of the track which had previously been destroyed. I was so sandwiched between other people that when I lifted one foot to change positions, there was already some other foot on the vacated spot. I was so pressed by the other passengers I could not even move my arms from my side; I wanted to light a cigarette but could not.

The small locomotive could hardly move the heavy train; it had to stop from time to time to build up more steam. In this way we moved slowly from one station to the next, through Prerov and Olomouc. Before we could get to Ceska Trebova we had to go back and, after a longish wait, the engine was changed for another stronger one. The first was not capable of pulling the train up the hills of the highlands. We stopped once again; we had to traverse a deep valley on a newly completed wooden bridge, and we were the first train to test it. We crossed over it only at walking speed and could hear the beams creaking underneath us.

The night fell slowly. For the whole day I had nothing to eat or drink. My sandwiches were in my suitcase somewhere at the far end of the coach, and I was still wedged in amongst the other people in an unchanging position. I dozed from time to time, standing. It was far from a real sleep, more like a switching off of consciousness through tiredness.

Anyway, I could not fall down.

After we had crossed over the highlands, the train ran more speedily, either because of the stronger engine or because of the better condition of the track. So we left Pardubice behind us, and after midnight we were in Kolin. The train stopped there for some time. The express from Jihlava should come through and we would be in its way if we continued. Many people left our train. At last I could breathe freely, but somebody told me that it would be better to change onto the express, so I found my suitcase and pictures in the corridor amongst the other baggage at the end of the carriage and I also left the train.

By then I was already over my hunger, only very thirsty and longing to spend a penny. There was such a queue in front of the lavatories that I went to the end of the platform and sprayed the rails there. I drank some water from the fountain on the platform and wished that I could huddle up or at least sit somewhere, but all the benches were full of sitting or lying people. Many were even sleeping on the platform itself. I found a free spot on which to stand my suitcase and sat carefully on one end of it, put my pictures in front of me, leaned my arms on them, laid my head on my hands and so relaxed. I even slept for a while, but I was awoken by the call that the express would arrive on the other platform.

A small panic started. I was carried along by a crowd of people, led to the stairs of the subway with such force that, loosing my footing on the stairs, the pictures nearly dislocated my shoulder, but I arrived on the correct platform. The express was just pulling in. When it stopped the door of one carriage was directly in front of me so I was the first to get in. The compartments were full, but the corridor was half empty. I leaned the pictures against the wall and once again sat on my suitcase. Nobody asked me to pay the extra charge for the express. In fact nobody throughout the day had even asked me if I had a ticket at all.

Thus I went to Prague. We arrived at 2 a.m., so my travelling had lasted twenty-two hours. In that time I had eaten nothing except for a small piece of my sandwich during the last part of my journey in the express train; somehow I could not swallow any more.

So many people were sleeping on the floor of the entrance hall of the station that it was possible to walk only along a few narrow paths amongst them, and even so I had to step over outstretched legs from time to time. I did not much like the idea of going outside and so went from one hall to another hoping to find a bit of free space near a wall somewhere, but everywhere it was the same. People from all corners of Europe were lying there - those who were coming back from concentration camps or from work duty in the Reich, from German prisoner of war camps or from wherever the war had blown them against their will. Every possible language was being spoken there, the travellers were sleeping on bundles and sacks which contained all their possessions, some of them were dressed in parts of worn uniforms with puttees on their legs. One mother was feeding her baby at her breast. Not far away was lying a scraggy man with sunken cheeks covered with stubble and a fairly recently shaven head on which only now was hair starting to grow once again; his eyes, even in sleep, were hollow, and he clutched a small half empty rucksack to his chest with thin, boney arms. In one corner four men played cards. Two of them wore sheepskin hats and all were unshaven. If I had met them somewhere in the country I would have thought that they were bandits...

I left the station building. No trams were running at night. I crossed the wide avenue, into a small park which was sunk in total darkness, walking between the trenches which remained after the uprising. The dark was so intense there that I walked very cautiously, step by step, holding my suitcase in one hand and pictures under my arm, whilst keeping my other hand stretched out in front of me. Even there I found people sleeping, by stumbling over one of them. Then I avoided another trench by fortunately touching its soft raised edge with my foot so that I didn't fall into it, and at last reached some bushes on a gentle slope, feeling the slope with my feet and the bushes with my hand. Nobody was lying there. Thinking it would be safer there than in the open I lay on the ground, put my suitcase under my head and leaned my pictures against my back. Huddling up, I was asleep in no time at all.

I was awoken by a burning sensation around my neck and wrists. Was it mosquitoes, ants, or something worse? My neck felt as if it had been broken, the suitcase was too deep to serve as a pillow. I put my pictures under my head instead; they were on plywood so the bundle was not so thick. It still was not very comfortable, but better than nothing. I turned onto my other side, laid the suitcase in front of me, held its handle with both my hands, and fell once again into an uneasy sleep. Disturbed once more by the stinging insects, the pictures were too hard under my head, and I felt colder and colder. Even so I slept - at intervals - until awoken by the jarring sound of the trams. It was already light. I was shaking with cold, aching everywhere and surprised to find how many sleeping people were lying around me.

Rubbing my eyes, I went to the tram station - my first steps into the centre of Prague. Not wanting to disturb my unknown hosts so early in the morning, especially as it was Sunday, the more important thing seemed to me to first of all find the Academy. I learned that it is on the opposite side of Prague to Pankrac, where Mr Vratislvsky's friends lived, and a tram from St Wenceslas Square would take me there.

Certainly the Academy would be closed on a Sunday, but I wanted to know where it was and what was the actual situation with regard to the examinations.

The tramcar was full. Somebody helped me with my suitcase and pictures. I was standing on the back platform, holding on tightly to avoid being shaken off by the movement of the tram - not yet knowing the necessary technique of balancing! Fellow passengers told me where to alight, and I went to the junction where the building stood - the Academy of Fine Arts.

The door was closed. On it was a notice that the

examinations would take place from 11th to 14th June. So they really would start tomorrow! I walked for a while, looking around, and at the end of the street went into a restaurant where I ordered a white coffee and ate the rest of my sandwich. The waiter - or the restaurateur - saw the bundle of my pictures and small suitcase, and he guessed the rest. From my accent he realised that I am from Moravia, and told me that his family originated there too. I asked him if I might leave my pictures with him and collect them next morning. He said he would gladly look after them for me, which was a great relief - travelling with the bundle was really uncomfortable.

With only my suitcase in my hand I went to have a better look at the school. It was a large building; where were the studios? I found them at the back, facing the park called Stromovka.

The quietness of Stromovka was balsam for my aching head. Between the trees and shrubs and by a pond with wild ducks I felt much better than in the streets which even on a Sunday were bustling and noisy. Everything seemed to me as in a dream, as if I were half crazy, not myself.

Here were grassy glades, trees, water - it was easier to breathe. There were even benches beside the paths. I sat on one, but soon my eyes closed and I was falling over. I turned round, stuck my legs under the back of the bench, with a piece of string attached the suitcase handle to a button on my jacket, lay my arms along the back of the bench, and rested my head on them. The sun warming my back, at last I fell into a comfortable sleep.

I slept for a long time. When I awoke some lovers were sitting beside me and it was clearly not all a dream - I *really* was in Prague. My hunger too was very realistic! I stretched my limbs, and sat down again for a while. Later I returned to the restaurant where I ate my lunch - cabbage with a double portion of potatoes and a small piece of meat. I drank some soda water, and bought two bread rolls and a slice of sausage for my supper, and was surprised how many food coupons they cut from my ration book. The restaurateur asked me if I had anywhere to sleep. I told him that I had, but in fact I thought that it would be better not to go to the photographer. I was horrified by Prague, and by the idea that I should undertake to cross the whole of the city not knowing if he would even be at home. It was a beautiful Sunday, and Mr Krejci would surely be out somewhere. And, after all, I would like to be as early as possible at the examinations in the morning, and who knows how I would manage to come right from the other side of Prague? There would certainly be crowds of people everywhere on a Monday morning when even on a Sunday the trams were so full. I decided to sleep in Stromovka. It was near, I liked it there and somehow felt more safe in the park. It was quiet, the weather was kind to me, and I could easily manage for one night. Sleeping on one of the benches again would not be so bad.

I walked and sat in the park all afternoon, admiring the beautiful trees growing on the greensward and watching the children feeding the ducks on the ponds. A lady was feeding the sparrows, tits and chaffinches, the birds flying onto and perching on the bench where she was sitting and taking the pieces of bread from her hand. Even a red squirrel hopped up to her for a piece of bread crust. It was as peaceful there as if the war had never happened, and almost as if it was not in Prague at all. The noise of the city came only as a deep, steady hum which retreated somewhere into a hardly noticable background - like the sound of falling water at Knezdub's little dam...

At evening people were leaving the park. Stromovka was emptying. Quite early on I chose a bench by a side path away from the pond, hoping the mosquitoes would not find me. As darkness fell I lay down, putting the jacket of my pyjamas over my shirt with my ordinary jacket over that, and from my pyjama trousers and towel making a small pillow to put under my head. The almost empty suitcase I tied with a string to the bench. I was so warm that there was no need to close my outer jacket.

I thought I had just started to sleep when somebody was shaking me.

"Here! Wake up! You are not allowed to sleep in the park!". It was a policeman or guard.

I sat up and said that I was doing nothing bad there, only wanting to sleep. He told me I ought to go to an hotel. I replied that, being in Prague for the first time and not knowing the city at all, I wanted to be near to the Academy where tomorrow I should take the entrance examinations. The man shone his torch on my pyjamas and said:

"If something happens, remember that I didn't see you here. You came only after my inspection at half past ten. Have a good night!" The torch was switched off, and I heard his receding footsteps. I lay down again, and slept as if I had been drowned.

The singing of the birds - sparrows, chaffinches and especially blackbirds - woke me at sunrise as they began a new day. Had they been singing so much during the war as well? After a bit the chorus quietened, and I fell asleep again.

Later, feeling much better, I washed myself in the pond, put the towel and pyjamas in my suitcase and left Stromovka.

It was still too early. I was hungry and very thirsty. My last drink had been yesterday with my lunch. The restaurant was still closed, and the Academy also. The exams would start only about 9 o'clock so there were more than two hours to fill. I turned my footsteps towards the sound of the tramway along Belcredi Avenue, and finding an automat which was open, I had my breakfast there and drank two cups of 'erzatz' tea. Exploring further, I reached the edge of the Letna plain. There were trenches there. I skirted round them onto the hillside which ran down to the river Vltava, and in front of my eyes there opened an astounding and breathtaking view. So *that* was Prague!

To the left, beyond the river over which stretched several bridges, lay a sea of houses and many towers. To the right there rose the panorama of the Castle, illuminated by the sun. I sat for a long time, just looking. I had never seen anything like that before, and somehow lost all track of time. If I succeeded in the exams what would be awaiting me here?

The exams! I had nearly forgotten them! I hurried back, but in my haste mistook the streets, could not find the Academy and had to retrace my steps before I could find the restaurant and collect my pictures. At last I entered the building with them.

The hall was already full of people. I completed the necessary documents, handed in my pictures marked with my name and number, and mixed with the other hopefuls.

The studios were on two floors; in each were two or three models, and painters both young and old crowded round them. The proposition was drawing of the head. Those nearest to the model were sitting on wooden boxes, 'practicables', and were drawing on large pads of paper balanced on their knees. Others were standing at easels on which they had sketchbooks or paper fixed onto boards. Most of them were drawing with charcoal, some with sticks of red or brown pastels. I had brought from home only a small sketchbook and soft pencil, and I could hardly see the models for all the other people.

There was no easel left for me, nor even any of the boxes, and it was not possible to draw just so, standing. So I went along to the next studio, but it was full too. I had been awake so early, and yet had come so late!

Just then some officer in uniform came along. He was in a similar situation as I, but he was more forceful than I. He collected from somewhere two of the boxes, handed one of them to me, and led me to a model at the end of the studio. There were just two places left for us, even though we could only see the model between the heads of other people. I was sorry to have wasted so much time there above the river, observing the city.

I had had no experience in drawing portraits. Nobody had taught me anything about how to do it, and from living models I had only drawn Tatinek and Maminka when during the few days of the battle for Bzenec we could not go out of the house.

Because I didn't know anything about drawing heads, it did not seem at all difficult to me, and I finished four or five drawings in the time when the others were still playing with their first.

Whilst we were drawing my officer neighbour was talking with me. Somehow we became friendly with one another, and at midday he took me to a better restaurant for lunch. He was a colonel and during the war had been commander of a large unit of partisans in the Czech-Moravian highlands.

After lunch we went back to the school. We drew two or three more heads, and then thought that that was enough. It was a beautiful sunny day. We both came to the same conclusion - that we could not hope too much that we would be amongst the 150 pupils who should be accepted. About 500 applicants had been taking the examination, and many of them clearly had had much more experience in drawing than we. Petr said it would be a pity if I had wasted my time in Prague, and so that I would have some pleasant memories of these days, he wanted to take me to Hradcany - the Castle. I picked up my suitcase and we went to see something of the Prague which I had been admiring so much that morning.

There I saw with my own eyes the granite monolith from the quarry in Mrakotin, and the gigantic flag poles from the firs cut from the virgin forest at Boubin, about which our schoolmaster in the elementary school had told us.

The Cathedral of St Vitus made an unforgettable impression on me. The stained glass windows by Prof. Svabinsky were, on that sunny day, shining like precious stones, and in the 'Descent of the Holy Spirit to the Virgin and Apostles' it really looked as if flames were leaping and glowing around the heads. I felt in that vast space the pulse of the thousand years in which our history had been developing there. I myself was walking on the ground where St Wenceslas had knelt in prayer, as had his admirer King Charles IV and the other Czech kings who were now laid here in their final resting place, and where millions of people had brought their thanks, pains, distress and prayers - "St Wenceslas - do not let us perish, nor those who come after us!". This mediaeval prayer we had sung ourselves during the difficult years of war, and our prayers had been fulfilled.

The door of the chapel of St Wenceslas was locked, but at least I was able to touch its romanesque bronze ring on which had rested the hand of our dying King/Saint.

We went out once again into the sunshine and drank some beer in the famous little restaurant 'At the Vicarage'. Then Petr accompanied me on the tramway to the National Museum where he put me onto another tram which would take me to the Pankrac district. The conductor would tell me where I should get out to look for Mr Krejci.

The station was called 'In a glade'. Such a pleasant name! Would it be a good omen for me? With the help of passers-by I found the right street. I was expecting to find a photographic studio there, but the house with the right number was just an ordinary house. However, in the corridor on the first floor was a letter box with the name *Krejci*. I found the door of the flat and rang the bell.

The door was opened by a young lady, Mrs Krejci. I introduced myself, explaining briefly who had sent me and why, and gave her the letter from Mr Vratislavsky. She was clearly confused by my arrival, but she invited me into the kitchen, where there was a baby in a cot. After reading the letter she told me that she was alone at home, that her husband was employed in Litomerice and came home only at the weekends. Their flat had only the kitchen and one bedroom. I said that I needed somewhere just to sleep for the next two or three nights, that anywhere would do - the floor in their anteroom would be quite all right if she could kindly lend me something soft to put under my head and a blanket with which to cover myself. Mrs Krejci said she would telephone her husband and see what he advised and, taking the letter with her, she went out of the flat, leaving me in the kitchen with the baby.

After a while she came back, clearly reassured. She said I could stay with them and could sleep in the bedroom on her husband's bed. I was very grateful to her; the bed would certainly be better than the bench in Stromovka! She wanted to prepare some food for my supper, but I told her that I really only wanted lodging for the night and would have my supper in the restaurant which I had seen just across the road from the tram stop. So Mrs Krejci gave me the keys of the house and flat. I left my little suitcase which had been accompanying me all the time like my shadow and went out.

When I came back we talked for a short while, and then excusing myself, I washed properly in the bathroom - at last even being able to clean my teeth! - and went to bed. I woke only when Mrs Krejci lay on the bed beside me, but in a moment was asleep again.

In the morning the smell of coffee woke me, the lady was already in the kitchen feeding her baby, and my breakfast was waiting on the table. I protested that I would buy something in town, but she told me she could not let me go out hungry,

This time I was able to go into the street with only my sketchbook - without my suitcase. It was such a relief!

That day too, at the school, the heads were once more our subject for drawing, and I was glad to find Petr there again. During the morning a professor came into the studio, walking from one to the other and occasionally exchanging a few words. When he stopped beside me he said:

"It is not clean - you should be shading by hatching, not by blurring!".

That didn't encourage me very much, but I changed my 'technique' and tried to do the hatching as he said. It certainly looked better somehow, but the blurring with my finger was much quicker and this time I finished only two drawings in the whole morning. After lunch with Petr I added two further drawings of heads, and then we again left together, this time to go near the National Theatre in the centre of the city. From there we walked along the embankment of the river Vltava to the Charles Bridge.

In front of me was the view of the Castle, Hradcany, which I had seen so many times in paintings and photographs that it seemed to me as if I had already walked there sometime in the past.

The Charles Bridge was a real gallery of baroque sculptures. Amongst the thirty sculptural groups I recognised the one of the Crucifixion in which, in the battle for Prague during the wars with Sweden, the Swedes had shot off Christ's head. I knew the scene from a coloured print which we had had at home in my childhood - 'The citizens of Prague defending the Charles Bridge against the Swedes in 1648'.

Another group, with St Luitgarde, looked as if the figures had changed to stone in that moment, as if not long before they had been in movement. They were still living, with their beauty transformed into stone.

We went under the Bridge Tower, and there opened in front of us the Lesser Town Square, dominated by the Church of St Nicholas, the baroque jewel which seemed to be in movement too as it grew upwards behind the little houses clustered in the foreground. There was some tension and yet harmony, both at the same time, between its wide green cupola and its pointed tower.

We went into the church, and it was as if we had entered into another, magic world. The altars, gigantic sculptures, pictures, frescoes, all joined with the columns, pilasters and ledges taking one's eyes higher and higher to the illuminated cupola covered with a painting in which the figures really seemed to hover in heavenly space. Only the glorious sound of the organ was missing... We stayed a long time, with so much to see and feel there.

To recover from all these impressions we went into one of the gardens above the Lesser Town. We sat on a bench, looking at the panorama of Prague, and Petr pointed out and named for me many other buildings, towers, churches and bridges on the river. I told him how grateful I was that he gave up so much of his time to me and that he was accompanying me on my first - and probably my last - steps through Prague, because after what I had just seen in the church of St Nicholas my hopes of success in my exams for the Academy were considerably diminished. Also I told him about my life up till now, about my first steps in painting, and that I did not know what to do if I were not accepted at the School.

"I would like to help you," Petr said unexpectedly. "I will give you a certificate to say that you were in my partisan unit. You never know when it might be useful to you." With surprise I told him that I had never been a partisan, and could never lie to anybody. Petr replied that many people would wish very much to possess such a certificate.

"But I don't know the Highlands where your unit was involved at all," I said.

"It doesn't matter. You could have been working as an orderly not as a fighting partisan. If you have the paper nobody will ask how it really was, and nobody will search for the details. It is possible that you will never use the certificate in the whole of your life, but you would have something in case of need and it could be of help. Fate sometimes plays strange games with us. Think about it and tell me your decision tomorrow."

We went to St Wenceslas Square again, and there we parted company. I went on to Pankrac and stopped at the restaurant for my supper. I had plenty of time to think over Petr's offer but, look at it from every possible aspect as I did, the result was always the same: I could not accept the certificate. In all probability I would never use such a document even when it was really my last chance. It was totally against that which had been engrained in me since my earliest childhood - *Never Lie!*

That night I didn't sleep very well, hearing the regular breathing of Mrs Krejci lying near me, and thinking about Petr's offer, about the impressions of the day, and about my future life. It seemed to me impossible that I would pass my Academy examinations successfully, but I could not imagine that my destiny was to spend the rest of my life sitting in some office.

Next morning I left the house feeling sleepy and depressed, and on arriving at the Academy even the last of my hopes vanished.

Our task was to draw or paint our own composition. Many of those in the studio were drawing or painting big pictures with many figures, motifs taken from the Prague barricades, welcoming the arrival of the Russian liberators, or large canvasses with landscapes. I sat there hopelessly, a pencil in my hand and a small sketchbook on my knees.

I walked through the other studios, but should not have done so. What, in fact, could I look for amongst those painters, some even professionals and in their fifties who had come there because they wanted to add to their title the name 'Academic Painter', 'Meister'? Even most of the younger applicants already had behind them some private or middle school artistic training. I was one of the youngest and had come here as a complete greenhorn. I found Petr and told him:

"I was thinking so much about your offer, but cannot accept it."

"We will talk about it outside," Petr interrupted me.

I started to draw, but in my head was a vacuum such as I had had in the Gymnasium when supposed to write a French composition. Tearing off two sheets from my sketchbook, I threw them away. On the third, painfully,

I exuded 'The Forest by Moonlight'. knowing that the drawing was very bad, but feeling resigned in some way. Possibly I should not have gone to the church of St Nicholas yesterday.

I handed in all my drawings. It was useless to continue.

After lunch Petr and I went to the Old Town where were the burned remains of the Old Town Hall. Even the gothic part with the old astronomical clock was damaged, and the 15th century clockwork was in ruins. We went into the Tyn church. Two foreigners were looking at the tomb of Tycho de Brahe, otherwise only Petr and I - and the silence - were there. We sat on one of the benches, and Petr said to me, whispering:

"I have the papers here. They are already stamped. They only need to have your own dates filled in and some details on which we must agree. Don't you really want them?"

"Not really. I don't know how to handle such things. Maminka always recognised, right from my earliest childhood, when I tried to deceive her. I think I will follow President Masaryk's dictum - *'Truth Wins'*. Anyway, it could bring many troubles to you too sometime in the future.

"I thought that was likely to be your answer, but believe me that things will develop here somewhat differently to the way you expect, and the truth does not always win. After all, even the truth can be seen differently from different aspects.

"You will not believe how many people have already asked me for the documents, even offering money for them, but I have thrown out most requests. Once it was a butcher who had been profiteering throughout the whole war from whom, because we were hungry, we had taken one stick of smelly salami and who was now claiming that he had been supplying provisions to the partisans.

"Another such 'worthy' was one in whose barn we had hidden a wounded man to whom we secretly brought a doctor at nights. The farmer learned about the wounded man only after he had already been moved away, but now wanted to be 'in the uprising' because, he said, he had given us a safe place for our 'hospital'. The doctor who had operated on the casualty to remove the shell splinter and sewed him together, so saving the man's life though in very real danger of losing his own if the Germans had discovered that he was helping partisans, at the end had just waved his hand and said that he had only been doing his duty.

"Unfortunately to some I had to give the papers, even when they had nothing to do with the uprising and it was against my will - but they were 'recommended' from higher up. Some of them I never even saw. We, too, had imagined at the time that it would be different. Now politics enters into everything."

We went out again into the square, full of sunshine, and from there continued through the zig-zagging narrow streets of the Old Town in which in some places there were still piles of cobble stones, remains of the barricades. I felt completely disorientated there, but at last we unexpectedly came to the river, near the bridge over which I had travelled each day to the Academy, and took the tramway back once more to St Wenceslas Square.

We parted near the Museum; would we ever see each other again? The examinations were finished. The results would be announced in a few days' time. Perhaps we would meet then. I thanked Petr. How would I have managed here without him? We embraced as if we had known each other for years. Petr got into his tram. He waved to me from the window...

Next day, 15th June, I thanked Mrs Krejci for her hospitality and went by train back to Bzenec.

On 18th June Stana went to Prague to register as a pupil at the High Technical School. He returned home with the news that on 20th June I had been accepted at the Academy.

Only later did I learn that I had been admitted as a pupil at the Academy's School of Painting through the vote of our great portraitist Professor Nechleba, who thought that my self portrait, which I had painted two years before and brought amongst the pictures with which I had supported my application, showed something worthy of encouragement and felt I should be given a chance.

To Mr Vratislavsky, who had made it possible for me to stay in Prague, I gave the small picture of the silver birches. He liked it especially and wanted to have something from me as a souvenir, thinking that we were not very likely to meet again.

I stayed at home only for one week as lessons started at the Academy on 25th June. Even during that week more landmines exploded in the vineyards. The war still continued here, and more people died.

We were packing for our return to Znojmo; it was my last week in Slovakia. I had to part with my magical waters, charming meadows and scented forests, and with the huge vault of the sky over that blessed country.

I left for Prague and never went back there again...

EPILOGUE

Almost seven years passed between the time when our country lost its independence and the ending of the war. During this time I grew out of my boyhood, an uneasy growth under conditions which sometimes made everything seem hopeless, with shortages and stringencies of all kinds, moving from place to place, the division of our family and in growing fear of the consequences of the inhuman, monstrous, perverse and sadistic behaviours of the Nazi occupiers.

People can and should forgive, but they should never forget that the Nazis were building their 'Reich' to last for a thousand years through murder, outrage and terror. Just as they murdered 6 million Jews in their elimination camps, so they also wanted to finish with the Slavs - Poles, Czechs, Slovaks, Yugoslavs, Bulgarians and Russians - wanting to make the lands of these peoples into 'room' for Germans. The Slavs were for the Nazi 'supermen' a lower race, with only one right - to slave for their masters. Hitler wrote in his book, the Nazis' bible 'Mein Kampf', that the Slavs are only a little less repulsive than the Jews, and he planned in time to eliminate them too...

It is possible and necessary to forgive, but it is not possible to forget the concentration camps, - Terezin, Dachau, Buchenwald, Auschwitz, Belsen, Majdanek, Osvetim, Treblinka, Sobibor and others - and the gas chambers and crematoria in which perished millions of fathers, mothers and children whose only guilt was that they were born into 'unclean' races.

It is not possible to forget the further millions of murdered 'enemies' of the Reich throughout Europe, including the 15,000 Czechs executed for 'countenancing the assassination of Heydrich' and the 116 inhabitants of Bzenec, killed in concentration camps where the Nazis took everything from them, even their names, substituting numbers tatooed on their forearms so that they would be easier to subtract. It is not possible to forget Lidice and Lezaky, Czech villages of 517 inhabitants, from which all men from the age of 16 were shot dead on the spot, all women transported to elimination camps, and most of the children killed with exhaust gases, while their villages were destroyed, flattened and wiped from the map.

Czechoslovakia was liberated from the Nazi occupation only to become, as did also the other countries behind the 'Iron Curtain', an exploited colony of the Soviet Union, which ruined our prewar rich and flourishing country economically, and our attempts to gain freedom were suppressed by military force, tanks, shooting, arrests and a new occupation.

Another forty five years were to pass before the Berlin Wall and Iron Curtain fell...